What people are saying about

God Interrogated

God Interrogated is a remarkably broad-ranging and erudite examination of the idea and experience of God, through the lenses of monotheistic religion, Western philosophy and science. It is an important new resource for those who are looking to make sense of God in a historically informed and non-dogmatic way. I can see it being of particular interest to people who are, like myself, from cultures that are rooted in the Christian tradition who are seeking to make sense of how God fits with science and rational philosophy.

Dr. Oliver Robinson, Associate Professor of Psychology, University of Greenwich

Lynne Renoir has created an astonishing tour de force, thoroughly exploring attitudes to God from philosophy to theology and even quantum physics. This book will give you a grounding in many areas of human thought and help you with our own inner journey.

Dr. Manjir Samanta-Laughton, author of *Punk Science* and *The Genius Groove*

God Interrogated

Reinterpreting the Divine

God Interrogated

Reinterpreting the Divine

Lynne Renoir

Winchester, UK
Washington, USA

JOHN HUNT PUBLISHING

First published by Christian Alternative Books, 2023
Christian Alternative Books is an imprint of John Hunt Publishing Ltd.,
No. 3 East St., Alresford, Hampshire SO24 9EE, UK
office@jhpbooks.com
www.johnhuntpublishing.com
www.christian-alternative.com

For distributor details and how to order please visit the 'Ordering' section on our website.

ISBN: 978 1 80341 172 9
978 1 80341 173 6 (ebook)
Library of Congress Control Number: 2022931037

A CIP catalogue record for this book is available from the British Library.

Design: Stuart Davies

UK: Printed and bound by CPI Group (UK) Ltd, Croydon, CR0 4YY
US: Printed and bound by Thomson-Shore, 7300 West Joy Road, Dexter, MI 48130

Contents

About the author

Philosopher Lynne Renoir questions the traditional view of God as an all-powerful being who created the universe and governs it according to his will. She argues that such an idea can be challenged philosophically, and that it does not accord with discoveries in modern science. On the other hand, she suggests, it is evident that experiences of transformation can occur in the lives of individuals who wholeheartedly embrace religious beliefs. Her book explores possible explanations for this situation by proposing that truth is found in the inner dimensions of a person's being, and is not something that can be imposed from an external source. Renoir's work was the result of her own difficulties in experiencing the transformation she sought through her Christian faith, and followed years of research undertaken in the areas of philosophy, science, and psychology.

Sydney 2020

The author can be contacted through her website:

lynnerenoir.com

Introduction

Among the most important questions that have ever been asked are those concerning the way everything we know came into being, and how this process or event may be related to the purposes of our existence. Three major religious traditions known as monotheisms attribute the whole of reality to a divine, all-powerful Creator. The earliest, Judaism, holds that God revealed himself to the Israelites, and that if they obey his laws, he will acknowledge them as the people he has chosen to bring his light to the world.[1] Christianity teaches that God came to earth in the form of his son, Jesus of Nazareth. Through faith in the saving death and resurrection of Jesus, it is claimed, our relationship with God, broken due to our sinfulness and rebellion against him, can be restored. Within Islam, the name of the one true God is Allah, and the Quran is his most perfect revelation. Muhammad is the final prophet sent by Allah to teach human beings how to live.

The decision to believe in God may result from a sense that there must be a higher power who is responsible for everything that exists. Alternatively, it may arise from an instinctive feeling that there is something more to life than can be explained by what is immediately apparent. Belief in God may also be based on the awareness of deficiencies in a person's experience. Among the needs that could be met in this context would be a sense of having sins forgiven, of receiving divine love, guidance, and protection, and of finding meaning and purpose in life.

Although the existence of God cannot be proved, a person who decides to exercise faith in him would expect to receive an assurance that some kind of transformation has occurred as a result of taking that decision. It is possible, however, for a person to accept the doctrines of a given faith and to put into practice the behaviors it requires, without at the same time experiencing any deep-seated sense of inner change. If on the other hand such an awareness should become a reality, the individual would have reason to regard the experience as a confirmation of the teachings embraced.

One of the factors working against the validation of beliefs by personal experience is that similar kinds of transformation can take place in the lives of adherents within the different traditions. Although there are certain areas of commonality among the teachings of the monotheisms, a comparison of specific doctrines shows that many of them are contradictory, or at least inconsistent, so that what is held to be true in one system of belief would be regarded as false in another. An example would be the Christian doctrine that God became man in the person of Jesus, whereas the idea of an incarnated God is regarded as blasphemous in both Judaism and Islam. From this it follows that if similar kinds of inner change occur in the lives of believers from the different faiths, transformative processes based on truth would appear to exist alongside those based on untruth. Because of the distinction between the experiences themselves and the concepts on which they are based, inner change of itself is insufficient to establish the accuracy of the beliefs held, regardless of the status attributed to them by the individual.

My own interest in this subject arose from fifty years of deep commitment to the Christian faith. Although I had no doubt that Christianity was true, I did not experience anything of the transformation that is described in the scriptures as being normative for the believer. During this period, I met people of various religious persuasions who were living examples of the qualities I lacked.

In a situation where I commit myself to belief in God, should I find that in the depths of my being I am not affected in any way, I am faced with two choices: one is to believe that my attempt to reach God, or to allow God to reach me, has been in some way defective; the other possibility is to form the view that there is no supreme being at all. In the former case, the reasoning processes that result in my acceptance of God's existence may cause me to continue with this belief. My position would be consistent with teachings in the various scriptures that human beings are affected by sinfulness or disobedience, so that an individual's experience could not be relied upon in making a decision about whether or not God exists. Although it would be possible for me to believe in an all-powerful being based on the evidence presented, in order to remain true to myself as a person who lacks the inner confirmation of belief, I may find it necessary to question the idea of the divine.

Whereas discussions about the existence of God are usually conducted at the level of the rational, the position outlined in this book is that the experiential dimension is of fundamental significance in determining questions of ultimate reality. It will be claimed that while experience can never establish the existence of something that cannot be proved, the presence of an inner transformative process is evidence of a form of truth that transcends the dimensions of right and wrong in reaching to the core of who we are.

The question of whether or not there is a God has historically been of interest to philosophers, and some of their positions are examined in the first section of this book. In contrast to science, which addresses questions of factual accuracy through the formulation and testing of hypotheses, philosophy examines all forms of human knowledge and experience, including the possibility of rational justification for belief in God. Examples of the issues discussed in philosophy that are relevant to questions about God's existence include the nature of reality, and how we are able to know anything at all, that is, whether we rely on our reason, the evidence of our senses, or our inner experience.

Until the modern era, which began in about the sixteenth century, most thinkers in the monotheistic traditions had some form of belief in an all-powerful being. Then followed a period in Western thought when the interpretation of experiences deemed religious, together with the earlier view that the concept of a supreme being was necessary to explain the origins of everything we know, came under attack from those who claimed that God's existence was not required to account for either the natural world or individuals' personal experience. In other words, they asserted that the idea of a supreme being had become irrelevant. Arguments have been advanced in recent times by theorists such as the philosopher Bertrand Russell and the biologist Richard Dawkins that religious belief is unscientific, misguided, or even dangerous. Associated with this position is the idea that human beings, particularly those living in democratic societies, have been emancipated from the constraints of authoritarian religious dogma.

While rejecting the above dismissals of God's existence, philosophers such as Jean-Luc Marion and Hilary Armstrong have argued that the notion of "God" is beyond human thought and language, and that it is inappropriate for the deity to be defined in the traditional way as a being possessing certain attributes. The approaches proposed by these thinkers, however, retain the view that humans can be in relationship with this ultimate mystery. Today there is an increasing interest in such an understanding of God, and it represents the continuation of a minority viewpoint that has always recognized the inadequacy of human attempts to comprehend the divine.

In most modern societies, truth is equated with the correctness of facts. This principle is applied to religious questions in the same way as it is to our everyday experience of the physical world. For example, the idea that there is one God, Allah, and that Muhammad is his prophet, is considered by Muslims to be a fact just as surely as is the idea that the earth is round. But in recent years, what have previously been regarded as the unassailable truths of our existence on this planet, have been shown to be enveloped in a fundamental ambiguity. It was originally believed that light consisted either of waves or of particles, but quantum theory has revealed that particles also have a wavelike nature, and that all matter exhibits both wave and particle properties. Because they have no definable location, the particles of which everything is made are seen as having an intrinsic connectedness. No ultimate separation can therefore exist between individual beings and objects.

After examining some philosophical theories about God, I will discuss the above findings in science and how they may relate to experiences recounted by mystics. In some of these altered states of consciousness, the awareness of self disappears, and there is no recognition of any identifiable being or object, everything being absorbed into a mysterious oneness. These experiences indicate a reality that seems to transcend the idea of a personal God, or even of a God who is beyond our ability to describe.

Having presented arguments from both philosophy and science that are mostly opposed to the traditional view of God, I will suggest that the question of the deity cannot ultimately be determined by means of reason or evidence, and that the experiential level of our being is the place where personal truth is found. For some individuals this will include a sense of connection with the divine, while for others it may involve the realization that we are one with the whole of reality.

We will start by examining the way philosophers have used reason to explore the question of whether or not God exists, and the means by which a relationship with the divine could be established.

1 The masculine form of God is normally used in Judaism and Islam, though within Christianity there is a growing tendency to use the feminine. For convenience, the masculine form is used in this book.

Section 1

God and Philosophy

Chapter 1

The Role of Reason

In the history of philosophy, scholars have examined the place of reason in the formulation of religious ideas. This chapter discusses some philosophers from a Christian culture, most of whom place a high value on humans' rational capacities. They analyze the role played by reason in addressing the question of whether God exists, and the kinds of characteristics he may possess. Most of these thinkers are also concerned with the question of divine revelation.

Belief in God has historically been concerned with the nature of his relationship both with the world and with human beings. In the seventeenth and eighteenth centuries it was thought that since the period of his original creative acts, God has had no continuing involvement in human affairs or in the functioning of the natural world. By contrast, certain modern thinkers known as process philosophers have suggested that God is not a separate, self-contained being, but is interdependent with the universe and evolves along with it. Traditional believers have generally taken the view that God is above and beyond what he has made, and that he desires to enter into a relationship with us, his creatures. To this end, it is claimed, he inspired selected individuals to write and teach about his will and purposes. The lives and testimonies of these chosen ones, together with the doctrines contained in their work, form the basis of the monotheistic belief systems.

Within Christianity, the various acts of divine inspiration involved numerous people over lengthy periods of time, and different perspectives are presented by the writers concerned. It is also the case that whenever the sacred texts are read, the kinds of life experiences people bring with them will give rise to a variety of interpretations in respect of the doctrines outlined. The historical consequence of this state of affairs has been the formation of various groups, each having a particular approach to the teachings as a whole. The question then arises as to the degree of liberty individuals can expect to be given when interpreting specific aspects of the faith. The Roman Catholic Church, which is the largest Christian body, has placed strict limits on what can be accepted in terms of an individual's insight into truth. At the other end of the scale are groups within the Protestant tradition who respect the autonomy of a person's relationship with God, including the exercise of conscience, and the possibility of truth being revealed through the private reading of scripture or through the testimony of others.

Following periods of persecution suffered by believers in the early history of the church, Christianity was given official status in the fourth century by the Roman Emperor, Constantine I, and became the dominant religion of the empire. From then onwards, the church and state were so entwined that with the rise of the Protestant Reformation in the sixteenth century, the persecution of non-Catholics was officially sanctioned. Many of the oppressed adopted a retaliatory approach, and later in the post-Reformation wars between Protestant England and Catholic Spain and France, people on both sides were killed purely on the grounds of their religious beliefs. A similar situation exists today in certain Muslim countries, where the death penalty is imposed on those who convert from Islam to another faith. As was the case in Europe, a particular interpretation of God's revelation is regarded as the absolute truth, and no provision is made for people to hold alternative views. The individual's rational capacities are thereby devalued, with disastrous consequences for the societies involved. Although the use of reason alone cannot establish the existence of God, it is one of the factors that is generally regarded as significant in evaluating the relevant evidence.

This chapter discusses the thought of the Western philosophers, Aquinas, Descartes, Locke, Leibniz and Hume. These thinkers examine the extent, if any, to which we can rely on reason to support the idea that a divine Creator exists and seeks to engage with us at a personal level. Later we will examine theories that give a lesser value to our reasoning capacities, or that elevate the role of experience above that of the intellect.

Seeking the divine

In the Ancient Greek world, myths were used to explain everything in human experience. Gods and goddesses, who were regarded as the personification of impersonal forces, were believed to exert their power over the world and its inhabitants. For example, Zeus, the king of the gods, had a protective concern for the socially vulnerable and was angered by evil deeds. Because his will was supreme, he was identified with the force of fate. Then from about the seventh century BC, the Greeks developed a unique way of questioning that sought impartiality in their attempts to understand their society, the world, and the universe. Having recognised that earlier religious ideas were merely products of artistic imagination, these thinkers aimed to replace the world of myth with an approach based on independent human thought. Their form of inquiry became known as philosophy. Among the questions they examined were the nature of reality and the means whereby knowledge is acquired. With regard to the former, it was typically assumed that matter had always existed in some form. While theories were developed to explain why the world exists, alters, and appears to us in the ways we observe, for most thinkers of this period, no all-powerful Creator was needed to explain how everything came into being.

Whereas the Greek philosophers had relied on reasoning to arrive at the truth, Christian thinkers of the medieval period taught that God reveals himself primarily in the scriptures and through the teachings of the church. But because of the high regard in which the Greek thinkers were held, attempts were made to reconcile some of their ideas with traditional religious beliefs, and thereby to provide "proofs" of God's existence. In the eleventh century, St. Anselm of Canterbury defined God as the greatest possible being we can conceive. If such a being were to exist only in the mind, he claimed, a greater being would be possible—one who exists both in the mind and in reality. From this he concluded that God must exist.[1]

One of the most significant contributors to the discussion of reason and revelation was the thirteenth-century theologian and philosopher Thomas Aquinas. An Ancient Greek thinker, Aristotle, had proposed that since movement occurs in the world, and the planets themselves are constantly moving, there must have been a "Prime Mover" who set everything in motion.[2] Aristotle also observed that everything in nature has a cause, which suggested the idea of a chain of causes stretching backwards in time. Since this chain could not reach to infinity, a self-sufficient "First Cause" was required to explain the existence of everything that is.[3] Aquinas equated this being or cause with the Judeo-Christian God.[4] A further claim made by Aristotle was that the basic nature of organisms is to fulfill their ultimate purpose or goal. This idea formed the basis of an argument demonstrating the existence of God that became known as the argument from design. It was claimed that the concept of everything in the world acting towards its own beneficial ends indicated the existence of a designer who has the characteristics of knowledge, purpose, understanding, foresight and wisdom. These various approaches to the natural world and their relationship to the Creator were accepted by most Western thinkers up until the scientific revolution which began in the sixteenth and seventeenth centuries.

In the teaching of Aquinas, the Greek view of the value of human reasoning can be placed alongside religious belief.

He proposed that everyone has a natural ability to formulate rational arguments for God's existence through observing the workings of nature. Then through a supernatural revelation, we are able to understand the qualities traditionally attributed to God, and the facts surrounding his entry into history in the person of Jesus. This knowledge is conveyed to us through the teachings of the church and in the scriptures. Although he gives recognition to the value of human rationality, Aquinas maintains that the exercise of reason alone is never sufficient to enable a person to have knowledge of the things God reveals about himself.

Most of the arguments for God's existence based on the role of reason concern impersonal characteristics and functions such as creativity, cause, and purpose. Even if these could be shown to have merit, there is no obvious way, other than by the acceptance of revelation, to connect the being they describe with the God depicted in the monotheisms as perfect, wise, gracious, loving, merciful, patient, forgiving and just, and as a being with whom we can have a personal relationship.

God's existence and clear ideas

Following the medieval period, there was a rapid increase in the exploration of the world, together with developments in the understanding of humans' place within the cosmos. Examples were the circumnavigation of the globe, and the planetary discoveries made by scientists such as Copernicus and Galileo. The hierarchies of the church became threatened by these events, since they seemed to imply that knowledge could be obtained purely through human thought and endeavor. As it turned out, this fear was well-founded. From the thirteenth century onwards in Europe, there was an increasing separation of rational thinking from belief in the authoritative teachings of the church.

A generalized uncertainty as to how knowledge could be

obtained eventually gave rise to a renewed interest in one of the Ancient Greek movements, skepticism, which denied the possibility of knowledge about anything whatsoever. As a response to the challenge presented by the skeptics, the seventeenth-century philosopher René Descartes attempted to show that some things can be established through the use of reason, including the existence of God.

Whereas Aquinas had suggested that the qualities of God can only be known through revelation, Descartes proposes that through the correct use of our intellect, we can be assured not only that God exists, but that he possesses certain attributes. Descartes' method is to doubt everything he has previously accepted, and on the basis of this approach, whatever remains will be revealed to be absolutely true and beyond doubt. He begins by doubting both the evidence of the senses and humans' powers of logic in areas such as mathematics. Descartes also posits the idea that an all-powerful Creator could have made us in such a way that we were deceived regarding our basic knowledge of the world. Alternatively, there could be an evil demon who was the cause of such a deception. Descartes' solution to the extreme form of doubt that would result from exercises of this kind is to seek a foundation for knowledge within the contents of his own mind. He reasons that the one thing he can never doubt is that he is thinking, since this is the case even when he is being deceived.[5] The performance of the attempt to doubt his own existence shows that his existence as a thinking being is itself beyond doubt. This conclusion he describes as "clear," in that it is manifest to his attentive mind, and "distinct," in that it is separate from all other ideas. Descartes then asserts that anything perceived clearly and distinctly by the intellect is true.

In the same manner as he knows his own existence, Descartes believes that he has a clear and distinct idea of the supremely perfect being.[6] His argument is that "God" represents something so perfect, that Descartes himself could not have been the cause of such an idea. Therefore God must exist as the only possible cause of the perfection contained in Descartes' conception of him. This conclusion is regarded as having the same kind of self-evidence as the facts of mathematics. Descartes also suggests that because he is limited and imperfect, he could not have created himself, since if he had done so, he would have given himself a perfect nature. The awareness of his imperfection is attributed to the idea that there must be a perfect being who has implanted within him the ideas of perfection and imperfection, since this kind of thinking would not arise from a human's interaction with the world. Furthermore, if God did not exist, Descartes' mind alone, he claims, could not have given him the kind of assurance he experiences that he has access to the truth.

A challenge to Descartes' argument is that people who are aware of self-evident or necessary truths such as those of mathematics, may not have a clear idea of a supreme being—or any kind of personal Creator. His theories in general cannot be detached from his experiences of life, not the least significant of which would be his religious upbringing, and the fact that belief in God was generally assumed in the society of his day. Descartes' basic spiritual orientation is evidenced in the claim he makes that God revealed certain things to him in dreams.[7]

A problem Descartes addresses concerns the fact that he sometimes goes astray in his thinking, but he reasons that God as the all-powerful being could have created him so that he did not behave in such a way. The explanation provided by Descartes is that he tends to exercise his will in relation to matters he does not understand. Yet he maintains that as long as he directs all his attention to a clear idea of God, he is not prone to any kind of error. Apart from the implication that his mind can reach a state of infallibility, Descartes' evaluation of humans' capacity to reason overlooks the opposing view contained in what is believed to be God's written revelation of himself. For example, in the Hebrew scriptures God describes his thought and that of humans as being separated by a gulf comparable to that between the heavens and the earth.[8] The reason for this gulf is that unlike God, humans are prone to sin, defined in a general sense as "missing the mark." This concept covers a range of behaviors—from inaccuracy of comprehension to acts of moral failing. The Christian scriptures (also known as the New Testament) carry a similar depiction of human limitations. These texts indicate that it would be impossible for human beings to avoid error completely, regardless of the diligent attention they may give to the idea of God. Since Descartes relies on the clarity of his thinking to demonstrate God's existence, his argument in this context is called into question.

The justification for Descartes' knowledge, he claims, arises from the workings of his mind, the senses having been shown to be potentially deceptive. He therefore needs a way to connect his clear ideas with the kind of reality existing outside his mind. Although Descartes attempts to prove the existence of God through the exercise of reason, in a later work he admits that what is divinely revealed is "more certain than our surest knowledge," and that these revelations are matters of faith and of the will.[9] Together with most philosophers of that period, Descartes used the discoveries in the natural world to demonstrate the power of the human intellect. Yet he also relied on the belief in God's involvement with his own thought process. Descartes ushered in what became known in the West as the period of rationalism, where there was a progressive decrease in traditional religious belief, and a corresponding increase in humans' confidence in their ability to master the world.

The individual and morality

While belief in God as the Creator had become integral to European culture, thinkers of the seventeenth century such as Matthew Tindal and John Toland advanced the view that the concepts of religion should be subjected to the kind of scrutiny that was applied to scientific theories. Anything that seemed irrational, or that in the end could not be proved, was to be eliminated from religious doctrine. Such an approach was given impetus by scientific advances, particularly those that benefitted people in their everyday lives.

A noted English philosopher of this period, John Locke, claims that all our ideas are grounded in experience, and that knowledge is determined by experience derived from sense perception. He also proposes that any given set of beliefs should be evaluated on the grounds of its effectiveness within a society. Locke stresses the importance of the individual in matters of faith and conscience, vehemently opposing the notion held in his day that political authorities had the power to legislate regarding beliefs. Because of his views on the freedom of the person, Locke argues that religious ideas cannot simply be inherited, but must be a result of individual inquiry,[10] and that a relationship with God requires the personal faith and commitment of the believer. The kind of faith Locke is discussing involves the exercise of reason and critical thought.

In contrast to Descartes' view that certain ideas are placed in our minds by God, Locke argues that if we already knew that God existed, we would lack the motivation to discover this reality for ourselves. Locke provides what he calls "proofs" for the existence of an all-powerful being.[11] In a version of arguments that had appeared in the thought of Aquinas, he states that the magnificent harmony and design of the universe reveals a God of wisdom and power, and he endorses the idea of the eternal God as the ultimate cause of everything that exists. Reason should also be used, in Locke's view, when addressing the question of divine revelation, particularly the supernatural events recorded in the Bible. It is only rational demonstration, he claims, that can validate the mysterious aspects of revelation, which means that the traditional teachings of the church must be supported by evidence.

According to Locke, the necessity for belief in God lies in the importance of morality, which is grounded in natural law, the law of reason. The indispensable role of God in the promotion of morality includes the system of rewards and punishments in the afterlife, where the final destiny of individuals is either Heaven or Hell.[12] (In some passages Locke modifies the idea of Hell, replacing the idea of eternal punishment with that of annihilation.) His position is that without threats concerning the afterlife, people would be disposed to act immorally.

Among the doctrines endorsed by Locke is that of salvation, understood as a saving from sinfulness. For this to occur, a person must exercise faith in Jesus as the "Messiah." This term appears throughout the Hebrew/Jewish scriptures, and refers to an expected king or ruler who would deliver the people from bondage to foreign rule. Within traditional Christianity, Jesus as the Messiah is regarded as the eternal Son of God, who secures for the believer a future in Heaven, and through whom sins are forgiven. Locke supports this conception of Jesus on the basis of the recorded miracles he performed. Although not endorsing the idea that Jesus was God, Locke affirms the historical fact that Jesus rose from the dead, as he considers a resurrected Messiah necessary to ensure life after death for true believers.

Morality for Locke is the supreme value, and he suggests that in an ideal society, it would not need the support of religion. From this it follows that if morality can be attained through the use of reason alone, the value of the Christian message is merely in its usefulness, the question of its truth being left undetermined. Despite his reservations about the faith, Locke holds that the advent of Christianity was essential on the grounds that no previous philosophy or religion had adequately addressed the human moral condition.[13]

Whatever Locke may believe about a God who is ultimately unknowable, it is not the God of the monotheisms. The idea of a punitive God is never balanced in his thought with the biblical idea of a loving God who enters into relationship with his creatures. Overall, the value Locke places on the exercise of reason with regard to morality tends to make religious belief superfluous.

Why does anything exist?

Reasons for belief in God include the idea that an all-powerful being would be required in order to explain how anything could come into existence, and in this context, the philosopher Gottfried Leibniz asks, "Why does something exist rather than nothing?"[14] In his view, the fact that there is a universe is a more perfect state of affairs than the possibility of nothingness. He claims that there is an infinity of potential worlds that do not become actual, since they lack the greatest degree of perfection. According to Leibniz, God has created the best or the most perfect of all possible worlds. He also suggests that an individual thing will become actual because it has a greater degree of perfection than something merely possible, and that only God, who contains within himself the reason for his own existence, could give potential things the urge to exist and thereby to come into being.

In dismissing the challenge that the best conceivable world would not contain evil, Leibniz argues that God created the world in such a way that evil is reduced to the minimum; whatever imperfections there may be, their purpose is to enhance the glory of the perfect whole. Various forms of this theory have been used by theologians over the centuries in their attempts to reconcile the idea of a loving and all-powerful God with the negative features of our existence, such as diseases and natural disasters.

Leibniz departs from Descartes' view that there are only two kinds of substance: the mental and the physical, or the mind and the body. The mind is nonmaterial while the body has extension—it fills up space. In challenging this distinction, Leibniz attempts to unite the mental and the physical by proposing that thought exists in matter. It was generally believed that an atom is the basic unit of matter, and that it gives rise to the existence of bodies, whereas for Leibniz, the universe, including every finite thing within it, is composed of an infinite number of what he calls "monads."[15] These are defined as non-physical points or centers of force. A living creature comprises a dominant monad, the "soul," together with a body consisting of subordinate monads, the dominant monad giving the organism its unity and identity. The question then arises as to how a body could consist of monads, since these have no spatial dimensions. Leibniz's answer reveals the two interdependent perspectives on which his philosophy is based: one is the material, and the other is the metaphysical, which involves the attempt to explain what is beyond our immediate understanding. When the latter perspective is used, monads are said not to exist in space or time, but from the former perspective, monads forming an organism are regarded as subject to the mechanical forces of the body.

According to Leibniz, the soul does not act directly on the body, as we might think would occur in an act of will, since monads are unable to communicate with anything external to themselves. The dominant monad cannot therefore influence the subordinate monads. Leibniz explains that God created a pre-established harmony so that the soul and the body are always in agreement; the development of the soul runs parallel with that of the body. Like the monads of which we are made, we ourselves have no direct knowledge of the world outside us; all we can perceive is our own being. Our comprehension of external things arises from the fact that what takes place in us is a mirror of what occurs in the universe. These facts are explained by the idea that God contains within himself the whole of reality. He is the primary unity from which all monads are produced. If this were not the case, things would be independent of each other and would not exhibit the order, harmony, and beauty that we see in the world, nor would we be able to understand the workings of nature. Leibniz contrasts his idea of a pre-existent harmony with the traditional view of a God who inserts his presence into human affairs, suggesting the image of a watchmaker who must continually intervene to repair the imperfect object he has made.[16]

The theory developed by Leibniz involves an original view of the relation between reason, science, and our knowledge of God. He claims that human reason, particularly as it is expressed in natural science and in the laws of logic, gives us an alternative route in understanding the divine. For example, although creation itself is a supernatural event, its truth is open to all rational beings and can be defended on scientific grounds. On the other hand, Leibniz explains that we cannot escape mystery. God as a supernatural, infinite being is beyond the comprehension of natural, finite humans. If, however, the mysteries of religion were irreconcilable with reason, and if we had valid objections that could not be answered, we would not find these mysteries incomprehensible but simply false. Among the religious ideas accepted by Leibniz that would seem to be beyond rational explanation are the divinity of Jesus and the Christian doctrine of the Trinity. Consistent with the significance he gives to the concept of perfection, Leibniz accepts the literal idea of Jesus' resurrection on the grounds that God could have enabled a human body to become "more perfect."[17]

Because of Leibniz's view that God does not intervene in the material universe or in the lives of humans, he regards the miracles recorded in the Bible as having mysteriously occurred already in the act of creation. He also considers that these miracles can often be explained purely on rational grounds, and that so-called "revealed" theology may eventually be shown to have natural explanations. The idea that everything in religion comes to us through revelation only rather than reason is challenged by Leibniz, but at the same time he does not subscribe to the theories of the philosophers known as deists, who rejected the very possibility of revelation. While the issue of mystery in a discussion of God has proved a barrier to some thinkers in acknowledging his existence, Leibniz believes he can reconcile such mysteries with reason. (In a later chapter we will examine theories that regard mystery, or in some cases paradox, as the only basis of true belief.)

Leibniz admits that some of God's ways are mysterious. Yet he is confident that God possesses certain characteristics, including the idea of being bound by laws that he cannot change. An opposing view was held by other thinkers of the time such as Robert Boyle, who argued that since God creates natural laws, he has the freedom to change them in any way he chooses, as occurs, for example, in the case of miracles. Whereas Leibniz accepts that miracles have occurred, and he describes some Christian doctrines as mysteries, as a rationalist he believes he can determine specific facts about God's capacities. In an imaginary discussion between Leibniz and Boyle, Leibniz would claim validity for his position on the grounds that his reasoning processes give him access to the truth about God and his unchangeable laws. But Leibniz would have to attribute to Boyle a similar ability to reason. The fact that the two philosophers reach different conclusions about the nature of God, indicates the extent to which reason alone cannot be relied upon in establishing any form of truth. Thinkers who regard the power of reason as the highest human attribute are unable to use this position to bridge the gap between the idea of a being who is necessary to explain the existence of the universe, and the personal God who is the foundation of monotheistic beliefs.

We know nothing

The philosophers already discussed offer various approaches in their quest to establish that there is a God, but there is no agreement among them as to whether the characteristics of such a being can be known. They also differ on the question of the relationship between the roles played by reason, revelation and experience. Factors that unite these scholars include their belief that a God of some kind exists.

A thinker whose views about the existence of God cannot be expressed in such a straightforward way is the Scottish philosopher David Hume. His basic theory of knowledge concerns what he calls "impressions." Some of these are received in the mind via the senses, and they seem to derive from our experience of the outside world. These impressions make a greater impact on our minds than ideas, and they are the basis on which ideas are formed.[18] In replacing reason with experience as the ultimate source of knowledge, Hume asserts that experiences in themselves cannot reveal truth, and that the errors we make arise from the limitations of our reasoning processes. Hume believes we are not able to know how sense impressions are actually caused by things external to the mind, and he shares a theory held by some philosophers that we lack proof of the existence of anything at all outside our own thoughts. The natural instinct we have to believe in the reliability of our senses, and to accept that the world would exist even if we were not here, is described by Hume as unavoidable. Yet he insists that it cannot be accepted as rational. Hume's skeptical approach to knowledge contrasts with the views of the philosophers discussed above, who in different ways are able to form conclusions about God, ourselves, and the world.

Hume examines various theories that were used to support the idea that through the use of reason we can determine that there is a God. He discusses the argument originally presented by Aristotle and affirmed by Aquinas, that in order to explain the chain of causes of things in the world, there must be an original cause containing the reason for its own existence. In challenging this position, Hume presents the following alternative explanations: God could exist without any cause; there could have been more than one Creator;[19] the universe may have always existed; it may have come into being without the need for any external causative factor.[20]

The whole concept of cause and effect is questioned by Hume in pointing out that we observe the conjunction of specific objects or events, where one is always immediately prior to the other. We then transfer past experience of these conjunctions into the future, but we have no knowledge of what is really occurring. Our belief in the principle of cause and effect enables us to function effectively; yet it is based merely on custom and habit. In any case, the idea of causation is confined to events in the world we know, and cannot be applied to a situation such as creation, which is outside our experience and beyond our comprehension.[21]

While Hume is clear in his denial of the causal argument for God's existence, he presents differing positions on the argument from design. In support of the argument, Hume describes the consistent patterns and orderliness of the universe, and claims that without this, scientific knowledge would be impossible. If we consider, for example, the structure of the eye, the idea that this orderliness is the work of a designer comes upon us with intense force. Hume also likens the world to a giant machine where all the parts fit together in a way that is beyond any human capacity, suggesting a designer with superior intelligence. Belief in such a being or deity is more reasonable than the idea of chance or the blind force of nature.[22]

Against the above approach, Hume argues that belief in God is not an instinct possessed by everyone, and that whatever reaction we may have when considering the origins of nature, it does not have an effect on us as strong as that of sensory impressions. Although we may possess a natural inclination to believe in a designer with intelligence, such a belief relies too heavily on an analogy with the way we perceive ourselves and our own capacities. The principle of attributing design to something made by humans cannot be applied to the origins of the universe, since the former can be explained by our experience in the world, whereas the latter is outside the bounds of that experience. If we have a feeling that a feature of nature must have been designed, we cannot extend this principle to the infinite universe, since that is something we as finite beings can never experience.

An issue that is basic to religion concerns the question of miracles, since they are used to support the view that there must be a God. The background to Hume's interest in this subject was a debate in the eighteenth century as to whether miracles could form the basis of religious beliefs. Some scholars adopted an argument presented in the Christian scriptures that if Jesus had not physically risen from the dead, as testified to by his disciples, there could be no grounds for the view that he was God incarnate. Hume rejected the very possibility that life could return to a corpse, since for him, experience is the basis for what we can know about the world, and events such as that described simply do not occur. The idea that the laws of nature could be suspended is interpreted by Hume as indicating an "interventionist" God rather than one who is responsible for the orderly functioning of the universe. While acknowledging that extraordinary events sometimes occur, Hume claims we cannot assume that natural laws would thereby be broken. It may be the case that what we thought was a law of nature needs to be adjusted to allow for perceived anomalies. The critical point for Hume is that we have no method of determining whether an unusual event is attributable to the activity of God, or to our limited understanding of nature.

Having proposed that the existence of God cannot be established through reason, Hume states that religion is inevitably based on faith. He also claims that if beliefs depend solely on revelation, they cannot be regarded as absolute truth. Hume rejects the medieval argument that the findings of reason can be added to those of revelation in order to validate a particular set of doctrines. Although Hume denies that belief in God is a fundamental instinct, he acknowledges that it is a tendency within human nature. He attributes this to the fact that we suffer pain and disappointment, and dread the inevitability of death. Our situation is exacerbated by our ignorance, leading to the belief that there must be an invisible power who is responsible for the way things are, and who can reveal something of himself and the purpose of our existence.

On the question of God's existence, Hume has generally been regarded as a skeptic He does not support traditional theism, but neither does he embrace atheism. His position is that what we know comes from our experience as sensory beings in a physical world. Since we have no direct contact with God at that level, the only way we can draw conclusions about his qualities is to imagine that he has characteristics like our own, though at an exalted level. This questionable form of thinking, according to Hume, effectively transforms God from that which is incomprehensible into a being more like ourselves.

According to Hume, a person who is moved by faith to assent to Christian doctrine is "conscious of a continued miracle in his own person" that goes beyond ordinary understanding. But because of his rejection of the possibility of the miraculous, Hume believes that such an individual would be suffering from some kind of delusion. On the other hand, since he does not endorse atheism, Hume's comments could leave open the possibility that if it should turn out that there is a God, people with a capacity for faith that is stronger than their belief in their own rational capacities may experience a sense of connectedness to such a being.

Summary

With the exception of Hume, the philosophers discussed in this chapter seek to demonstrate that through the use of reason, evidence in favor of God's existence can be drawn from factors such as the functioning of the universe and the nature of the human mind. Descartes claims an infallibility of thought under certain circumstances, but the problem common to all the writers is their inability to explain how rational thinkers can arrive at opposing points of view. The acceptance of revelation leads to the categorization of seemingly irrational concepts as mysteries. This approach enables the writers to uphold the value of reason, even when it is confronted with ideas that are beyond its powers to address.

The question of God's existence is sometimes linked to the qualities he is said to possess—in particular the idea that he is the author of moral standards. Failure to measure up to these standards is believed to incur God's judgment. Taking an alternative position, Locke proposes that morality can be acquired independently of religion, so religious beliefs could have no unique role in the promotion of moral behavior—other than the threats they contain with regard to the eternal punishment of nonbelievers. Leibniz raises the problem of how a perfect and all-powerful God could allow innocent forms of human suffering. But he seeks to defend God by arguing that the presence of this suffering is necessary for the ultimate good of humanity.

Hume contests rational arguments for the existence of God, together with the various claims made by theists that are outside the area of experience in the physical world. The reasoning capacities possessed by humans, according to Hume, cannot be linked to an unprovable and mysterious process of revelation for the purposes of establishing the existence of an all-powerful being.

The next chapter examines the role played by experience, and whether this dimension of our being can establish the existence of the divine.

1 Anselm, *Proslogion,* tr. Thomas Williams (Indianapolis: Hackett Publishing Company Inc., 2001) chs. 2 and 3.

2 *Aristotle Physics: Book VIII,* tr. Daniel W. Graham (Oxford: Oxford University Press, 1999), 8.6 258b10–259a19.

3 For Aristotle's complex discussion on the question of cause, see *The Metaphysics of Aristotle,* tr. Rev. John H. McMahon, (London: Henry G. Bohn, 1857), Book I, Ch. III.

4 *Thomas Aquinas, Summa Theologica: Vol. 1 of 10,* tr. Dominican Province, (Charleston SC, USA: Forgotten Books, 2007), 433.

5 René Descartes, *Principles of Philosophy,* trans. John Veitch (Montana: Kessinger Publishing, 2004) 17.

6 Ibid., 23.

7 Alice Brown, "Descartes's Dreams," *Journal of the Warburg and Courtauld Institutes,* 40, (1977): 256–73.

8 Isaiah 55: 8.

9 Descartes, "Rules for the Direction of the Mind," in *The Philosophical Works of Descartes,* tr. Elizabeth S. Haldane and G. R. T. Ross (1911; reprint Cambridge: Cambridge University Press, 1984), 1:8.

10 Locke, *A Letter on Toleration,* ed. James H. Tully, trans. William Popple, (Indianapolis: Hackett, 1983), 23.

11 _____, *An Essay Concerning Human Understanding,* ed. Peter H. Niddich (Oxford: Oxford University Press, 1979), I. 1. 5, 45.

12 _____, *A Letter Concerning Toleration,* (New York: Bobbs-Merrill, 1955), 46.

13 *The Reasonableness of Christianity* in *The Works of John Locke* (London: Otridge & Son et al., 1812), Vol. VII, 139.

14 Leibniz, *The Monadology and other philosophical writings* (New York: Garland Publishing Inc., 1985), 247.

15 ______, *Discourse on Metaphysics and the Monadology* (New York: Cosimo, 2008), 67.

16 ______, "Letter to Clarke," cited in Leslie Jaye Kavanaugh, *The Architectonic of Philosophy: Plato, Aristotle, Leibniz*

(Amsterdam: Amsterdam University Press, 2007), 252.

17 Academy of Sciences of Berlin (eds.), *Gottfried Wilhelm Leibniz: Sämtliche Schriften und Briefe*, VI, iii, (1923), 365, n.5, cited in Daniel J. Cook, "Leibniz on 'prophets', prophecy, and revelation," *Religious Studies*, 45, (2009), 278.

18 *The Philosophical Works of David Hume*, Vol. I (Edinburgh: Adam Black and William Tate, 1826) 15.

19 Hume, *Dialogues Concerning Natural Religion* (1779) in: *Dialogues and Natural History of Religion*, ed. by J.A.C. Gaskin (Oxford & New York: Oxford University Press, 1993), 68–9.

20 ____, *A Treatise of Human Nature*, edited by L. A. Selby-Bigge, 2nd ed. revised by P.H. Nidditch, (Oxford: Clarendon Press, 1975), 78–9.

21 ____, *Enquiry Concerning Human Understanding*, ed. L.A. Selby-Bigge (Oxford: Oxford University Press, 1966), Section XI.

22 Ibid., 135 and 143.

23 Hume, *Philosophical essays: on morals, literature, and politics*, Volume II, (Philadelphia: Edward Earle, 1817), Section X, 124.

Chapter 2

Examining Human Experience

The thinkers discussed in the first chapter address the question of human reason as the basis of knowledge, and the role the senses may play in this process. They then apply their conclusions in analyzing whether it is reasonable to believe in the existence of God. We will now consider three philosophers whose primary interest with regard to God is in the possibility of experiencing him in everyday living. Their views vary widely as to the characteristics such a God may possess, and the basis on which a relationship with him could be established.

The moral view

In the eighteenth century, Immanuel Kant introduced a new approach in examining reason and the senses, and he used his findings to argue that although we cannot prove God's existence, we can believe in him on the basis of our moral sense. For Kant, the central concerns of human inquiry are: "What can I know? What ought I to do? What may I hope?"[1] His major work, *The Critique of Pure Reason*, explores the boundaries of human thought, and he writes of "limiting reason to make room for faith."[2]

Whereas Hume had claimed that we have no absolute knowledge of anything at all, Kant proposes that there are some things we can know. His work seeks to determine what must already be the case in order for something to be possible. With regard to our understanding of the world, Kant argues that since we are able to have experiences, our thought processes must be structured in ways that enable these experiences to occur. To this end he proposes a list of twelve categories that organise our thinking. They include concepts such as unity, plurality, possibility and necessity.[3] He also holds that space and time are inner forms by which we are able to perceive things, rather than being independent features of an external universe.

Kant analyzes the philosophical problems arising from the traditional attempt to extend the forms of thought beyond their limits. Of particular concern to him are the medieval arguments for God's existence. St. Anselm defines God as the greatest being of which we can conceive, and then proposes that a God who exists as an actual being is greater than one who exists merely in the mind.[4] According to Kant, the existence of God cannot be regarded as a greater concept than the idea of God, since attributing existence to a being does not "add" anything to it, but merely indicates its occurrence in reality. Kant also rejects the argument about God as the "first cause" on the grounds that our only experience of cause relates to things within the world, as had been argued by Hume, and cannot be applied to the world itself. The medieval arguments as a whole are seen as invalid attempts to transcend the limits of our reasoning powers.

The basic position held by Kant is that for something to be knowable, we have to be able to describe it in terms of its properties or qualities, and that our knowledge of anything is limited by the structure of our thought processes. From this it follows that we do not have access to things as they are in themselves. Kant believes, however, that we must presuppose the existence of something beyond our experience of the world, even though we can know nothing about it. The basis of this presupposition is that the absence of anything outside our own perceptions would preclude us from making sense of our everyday existence. When it comes to the question of God, Kant asserts that this matter does not come within the ambit of his theory of knowledge, since we do not have access to the properties of God whereby the mind would be affected and its structuring processes activated. God is therefore classified in the same way as things in themselves; we cannot prove that he has any particular characteristics, or even that he exists at all.

Kant acknowledges that some aspects of experience may point us toward a belief in God. An example he gives is the kind of aesthetic experience relating to what he calls the "dynamically sublime."[5] It involves a sense of being overwhelmed by features of the natural world such as the ocean, volcanos, and lightning. Our reactions can lead us to assume that nature as a whole is the work of a great and wise being. A further indication of God's existence arises from the ability of human beings to acquire knowledge of the scientific principles governing nature. We could therefore conclude that a supreme being has created us with a capacity to explore what he has made. Furthermore, in the structure of natural objects and living creatures we find a harmonious unity, suggesting the idea of a God who is rational and purposeful. For Kant, such human abilities and the various features of the natural world point towards the possibility that there is a God, though they cannot be used to argue for his actual existence.

Having outlined the limitations of our knowledge, Kant believes we can have a kind of certainty that God exists. He argues that the idea of God must be presupposed in order to explain a particular aspect of our experience, even though any concept of the divine could not be regarded as a proof of his existence. The characteristic Kant refers to arises not from the exercise of reason, or from experiences that may overwhelm us, but from the fact that we have a moral nature and are able to make decisions as to how we should act in particular situations. Kant points out that we are sometimes torn between a desire to do something, and a deep sense that what we want to do is wrong. Such a feeling is not simply a personal perspective, but is based on what we believe would be the view of anyone else in our position who is seeking to do the right thing. What Kant describes as the "moral law" is that we should act in such a way that we would regard the motivating principle of our actions as being applicable to everyone in all situations.[6] If we disobey this law, our conscience can make us feel uneasy and even humiliated, but if we do what we consider to be our duty, we experience pleasure and gain self-respect. Kant interprets our sense of right and wrong as suggesting that there is a God who speaks within us by looking into our hearts and stirring up our moral sense.[7] Although this awareness of itself cannot be used to prove God's existence, Kant's own experience enables him to conceive of God as an "all-embracing, morally commanding, original being."[8]

In a major departure from traditional beliefs, Kant proposes that we do not understand moral duty on the grounds of what God is said to have revealed in biblical history. Instead, we believe something has come from God because we already know what our duty is. Our conscience is experienced as a kind of inner judge, who has the power to assess behavior as good or bad, and to issue rewards and punishments. Conscience is depicted by Kant as the voice of God within us. The assumption that God is both a moral and an all-sufficient being, while not constituting an objective or theoretical proof, is nevertheless subjectively sufficient as a moral proof.[9]

According to Kant, the purpose of God in creating the world is the realization of the "highest good."[10] Its primary element is virtue, the reward for which is happiness, defined as a sense of well-being and contentment, and a consciousness of the agreeableness of life. When human beings act in accordance with duty, they are seeking to become worthy of this happiness. For people who live this way, God desires that they should obtain happiness in proportion to their virtue. This world, however, is one where humans experience injustice and suffering, and the high demands of morality are greater than anything achievable in this life. Since no connection can be shown between happiness and virtuous living, Kant concludes that the highest good can only be achieved if there is a future life where God is able to secure the justice that is unobtainable in the present world. When we recognize our duty, and we are in harmony with the will of God, attaining the highest good becomes our greatest hope.

While the existence of the deity cannot be proved, Kant claims that God gives us sufficient evidence on which to base our faith. We have an inner hope and conviction that in the end he will reward our moral efforts. In Kant's theory, we must presuppose the existence of God in order to account for the possibility of ultimate happiness. Faith is defined by Kant as an experience of trust, so that whatever is meant by "God" must be worthy of that trust. Being able to ensure that our pursuit of morality is not a vain hope, he must be just, all-knowing and all-powerful. If this were not true, we would have to deny that our sense of morality is rational. It is only belief in God and immortality that gives meaning to our existence.

In summary, Kant's arguments concerned with limiting reason to make room for faith challenge attempts to prove God's existence. But he argues that our moral sense gives us a basis for faith. The idea that we cannot know anything outside the limits of our experience as creatures of space and time means that we are prohibited from saying anything definite about God, including the possibility that he actually exists. The arguments presented by Kant do not even amount to a view that the reality of God is probable. What is described as the divine is not directly knowable. It is rather the case that there are certain indications of something corresponding to such a being. Although Kant uses the personal pronoun when referring to God, he claims it is impossible even to establish that nature has only one Creator. Yet he asserts that the lack of proof that God exists cannot be a basis from which to argue for his non-existence. Kant's overall position is that we have no grounds for saying that God exists; we can only have a moral certainty of this idea.

Towards the end of his life, Kant claims to have had an experience of God, but he again rejects the idea that any such experiences could provide us with factual knowledge. He also states that after his death, he anticipates having to answer to the judge of the world regarding his life's work.[11] Regardless of the limitations on our ability to know anything at all, Kant regards his certainty that God exists as a feeling that is valid from the perspective of morality and duty. His writing reveals a personal commitment to the existence of God through the descriptions he gives of the relationship that is possible between God and the individual. On the other hand, his approach to the problem of knowledge means he is unable to affirm that the experiences he describes point to a reality that lies beyond the limitations imposed by the structure of our minds.

God beyond and within us

A challenge to Kant's views came from the nineteenth-century philosopher Edmund Husserl. His theory is that the basis of truth is our experience of living in the world, and that it is only by understanding how we make sense of anything at all that we can discuss what we mean by concepts such as God, religion and faith. Husserl began his professional life as a mathematician, but he decided to become a philosopher after reading the Christian scriptures. The powerful and transformative effect these writings had on him resulted in his desire to discover through rigorous inquiry "the way to God and to a true life."[12]

The thought of Husserl has a similarity to that of Kant in that he seeks to understand what must already exist in order for something to be possible. A major difference between the two thinkers is that whereas Kant denies that we can know things as they are in themselves but only as organised by our minds, Husserl claims that once we understand the way meaning is created, we can be confident that the things we perceive are the actual objects we take them to be. An example of the various ways we give meaning to an object is to grasp it as a unity based on the different perspectives from which it shows itself, and on the different points in time in which it is perceived.[13] Both thinkers use forms of human experience to suggest the possibility of God's existence, but unlike Kant, Husserl believes that philosophy and religious faith can work together towards an understanding of the divine.

Husserl outlines two approaches in discussing the existence of God: one is based on his own philosophical position; the other involves the experience of faith in God's self-revelation. In his philosophical approach, Husserl argues that the fact that we possess reasoning processes suggests the existence of an all-powerful and all-knowing being who created us with these powers.[14] A further aspect of Husserl's philosophical argument is the idea that everything in the world is directed towards actualizing its potential.[15] He applies this principle not only to the way organisms develop, but to basic instincts and unconscious movements, both physical and mental. Furthermore, human acting is driven by a desire for "what alone has in itself an absolute value."[16] It is only the infinite God who can be the foundation of meaning and purpose, guiding finite beings in their orientation towards the universal ideal of absolute perfection. Husserl describes God "as the idea of the most perfect being, as the idea of the most perfect life, which out of itself constitutes the most perfect 'world.'"[17]

From the perspective of his experience based on faith, Husserl proposes that consciousness has an immediate awareness of an absolute being. The effect of this awareness is to banish doubt and to provide a definitiveness that is not available to perception and reason. Such an experience of the divine is described as being more fundamental than any reasoning about his existence.[18] Husserl also presents two complementary views of God. These concern the question of whether he is wholly beyond us, but yet can be experienced as a power within us, or whether he is so completely identified with us—and in some theories with the world also—that he has no form of independent existence. In the former case he is described as transcendent, and in the latter case he is described as immanent.

The arguments outlined above in Husserl's philosophical approach include the idea that God has a guiding role in human behavior. In this context, the divine is depicted as transcendent. On the other hand, Husserl refers to God as "the unsearchable Within,"[19] suggesting the concept of immanence. For Husserl, "divinity is implicit in every act of consciousness." This indicates that what we take to be our own thoughts are actually expressions of the ideas God implants within us. The unity and purpose of the world and ourselves are seen as merely "dependent moments" in the infinite meaning-giving process. Our inseparability from God is further implied in the awareness we have that we are an embodiment of the divine light. This occurs when we act in ways that are noble and good. Husserl believes that humans contribute to the process of God's self-realization.[20] In fulfilling the divine will, we and the world "become God."[21] Contrary to traditional doctrine, Husserl writes that prayer should not be directed outwards, but inwards to the God within our consciousness.[22]

Religious faith is described by Husserl as the firm belief in the ultimate meaningfulness of our lives, even when we are confronted with a sinful, non-rational world, and when we experience suffering and misfortune. God brings happiness and fulfillment to those who believe that he exists, and that this world is his world. For Husserl it is only divine love that can completely fulfill us. Whereas we can use reason to argue that there must be a God, faith involves the kind of belief that goes beyond rational insight and arises from the heart and will. Husserl's claim is that God "works in the deepest roots of the authentic person who does not will anything but what is true, as that which we cannot let go of without being forced to give up our life as meaningless."[23] In a personal disclosure, he writes that to believe in the development of his true self, he must believe in God, and that in being faithful to absolute duty with all the strength of his soul, he experiences the guidance of God in his life.[24]

Husserl writes of the inner awareness of a transcendent being, and he believes that those who are open to the will of God are conscious of expressing the divine light, thereby finding ultimate meaning and fulfillment. Overall, Husserl's ideas about God depend on his belief in the self-revelation of God, and ultimately on his own personal experience of a relationship with the divine.

The death of God

An opposing position to that of both Kant and Husserl is taken by Friedrich Nietzsche, who examines questions of experience, religion, and morality. But rather than expressing an opinion as to whether or not God exists, he challenges Christian beliefs—in particular, its negative view of the human being. In place of the traditional concept of the divine, which Nietzsche regards as having lost its relevance, he expresses a desire for an experience of God that recognises humans' intrinsic worth. The ideas he proposes are set in the context of a discussion on morality and knowledge.

According to Nietzsche, our reasoning processes and our quest for truth cannot be separated from the personal meanings and values we hold. Any attempt to go beyond our own perspectives to a neutral basis of reality overlooks the fact that we can only believe in something that is already meaningful to us.[25] A consequence is that if we seek to understand things as they are, quite apart from our individual ways of thinking, a false contrast is created between what is actually there, and what is thought to be merely in our minds. Similarly, our meanings and values are not regarded as completely real. Rather than proposing ways to reconnect our experience to the supposedly real world, Nietzsche argues that the distinction is invalid in the first place, since the world itself contains everything we need for meaningful existence.

On the question of morality, Nietzsche compares people who allow values to be created for them, believing that these are true and applicable to everyone,[26] with those individuals who draw on their own moral capacities in creating values for themselves. He argues that because of the great variety in personality types, it would be impossible for everyone to conform to a given set of characteristics and ways of behavior. In Nietzsche's view, the desire for objective truth and universal morality is linked to belief in God, who is regarded as the ultimate standard against which our thoughts and actions are judged. He reasons that because people in the West are insecure, they seek an unchangeable truth on which they can depend. An associated belief concerns the existence of a world, usually described as "heaven," lying beyond our sensory perception.[27] The adoption of this questionable idea arises from the human desire to invent a place where we can be assured of the truth of our beliefs. Our present world is devalued in being compared with an unknowable, better world. "The vale of tears" where we now live is contrasted with the realm of eternal bliss on the other side. Everything in the world we know is rejected as sinful, and adds to the insecurity we feel about our knowledge as a whole.

One of the main problems with Christianity, as Nietzsche understands it, is the way it describes God as an immaterial pure spirit, in contrast to the human being who is trapped in the body and its sinful desires.[28] A consequent obsession with morality means there is no outlet for the natural instincts, which are thought of in terms of evil temptations. According to Nietzsche, the church has never asked, "How can one spiritualize, beautify, deify a desire?"[29] It has rather sought to repress or even eliminate the sensual. For Nietzsche, "an attack on the roots of passion means an attack on the roots of life," where it is regarded as something merely to be endured in anticipation of a better life to come. Conversely, self-denial can be a way of making life easy, in that it requires less effort to engage in a process of renunciation through unconditional obedience to a higher law than it does to work on the personality with which the individual is endowed.[30] To reach our full potential, we need to resist subservience to any superior power or given set of beliefs. Unquestioning submission to imposed moral standards can involve hidden feelings of pride, and an intolerance towards those who hold different views. While preaching love, the church has on many occasions engaged in torture, justifying such actions on the grounds that the souls of unbelievers must be saved from eternal punishment.

The position advanced by Nietzsche is that our life instincts point towards a healthy morality. When uncontrolled, the passions can drag us down, so we need to determine the appropriate outlets for their expression, refining them so that they add to our personal enrichment and our growth to maturity. Nietzsche defines the spiritualization of sensuality as love,[31] and he refers to the "unexhausted possibilities" within ourselves and the human world. For Nietzsche, Christian doctrine undermines our capacity to appreciate the intrinsic meaningfulness of human experience. On the other hand, when we use courage and discipline in the struggle against a hostile environment, we come to recognise that life itself has a purpose and meaning, and on that basis, we are able to develop qualities of character such as patience and moderation.

Nietzsche's approach to morality is also relevant to his theory as to how the idea of God arose. Primitive people, he suggests, had a sense of indebtedness to their ancestors. Then followed a period when this indebtedness was transformed into a fear of the gods, resulting in a variety of attempts to please them. But with the advent of the Christian God, people experienced guilt arising from a debt that could only be paid by God himself through the death of his son, Jesus.[32] This act of divine love, however, could not relieve the feelings of indebtedness. Instead, its effect has been to overwhelm human beings with a sense of guilt and worthlessness. In failing to meet the prescribed standards of morality, we compare ourselves with divine perfection. Seeing ourselves in a negative light, we become fearful of future punishment. Then when the feeling that we need redemption from sin or wrongdoing is met by the belief that God has forgiven us, we interpret this as an act of undeserved mercy. Yet we are never freed from our ongoing struggle with our sinful nature, and so we are always wanting and needing to be forgiven. This whole way of engaging with ultimate reality, from Nietzsche's perspective, is psychologically harmful.

A contrast is drawn by Nietzsche between what Christianity became from very early in its history, and the life and teachings of Jesus. The change is attributed to the apostle Paul, who wrote most of the books in the Christian scriptures. Whereas Jesus described a new way of living, Paul spent his energies teaching what he believed was correct doctrine. Nietzsche regards this shift of focus as the essential error of Christianity, where practices that are life-enhancing are replaced with rituals and dogmas. Paul is accused of rewriting the history of a man who died as he had lived—not to save humanity, but to show us how we should live. The teachings of Jesus concern the happiness that can be experienced in this life. Paul, on the other hand, promises untold joy after death, but only to those who believe in Jesus as the one who can save us from our sins. For Nietzsche, Jesus was a free spirit who rejected the legalities of religion, achieving a purity and completeness of personal life. Instead of resisting the false accusations and physical cruelty that was inflicted upon him, he loved and forgave his enemies. His teaching spoke of an inner light and a state of mind that is experienced by living a peaceful, judgment-suspending existence, free from worry, guilt, and anger.[33]

Nietzsche addresses the idea that in Western thought, God is no longer needed for the roles he has been accorded in the religious traditions.[34] His creative activity has been replaced by what is regarded as human progress. Nature ceases to be looked upon as a proof of God's goodness and care, nor is he considered to be the originator of a moral order in the world, or of an ultimate purpose for our existence. Humanity now depends on science to explain everything, but because the world is thereby reduced in status to a planet dependent on the laws of nature, it ceases to have any intrinsic worth. All we now have to sustain us is a set of bare facts. Nietzsche regards this situation as a crisis, in that nothing meaningful is able to fill the void left by the absence of God.

The remedy proposed by Nietzsche is that we need to find a God who epitomises the value of life itself. Although he rejected traditional theism, Nietzsche was also a critic of atheism. He had an incessant longing for the arrival of what he calls "the Unknown God."[35] The religious intensity Nietzsche possessed is revealed in a poem where he writes, "I want to know you, Unknown One, you who have reached deep into my soul, into my life like the gust of a storm."[36] What is envisaged would not be a law-giving, life-denying being from some other realm, but a God who brings us in this world abundant life, happiness and fulfillment. Nietzsche's desire seems to be for a God whose relationship with us is consistent with our experiences of living in the present world. Such a being would affirm our efforts in developing the qualities and unlimited potential with which he has endowed us.

Summary

Of the three thinkers discussed, two believe in some kind of divine being because of their own personal experience. For Kant, this experience is based in our sense of morality and the exercise of faith, whereas for Husserl, it is ultimately in the awareness of God's power and guidance in his life. Nietzsche rejects the God of Christianity, together with the doctrine of human moral failings and the threat of eternal punishment. Although he does not engage in a traditional form of debate about the existence of God, Nietzsche's idea of a different kind of deity changes the focus from a God who sits in judgment upon his creatures, to one who would validate that which makes us human.

We will now look at two philosophers who are deeply committed to the idea of God, but who reject the dependence on reason to prove the existence of a divine being. They apply unique kinds of experience in their attempts to establish that such a being must exist.

1 Kant, *A Critical Inquiry into Grounds of Proof for the Existence of God* in *Metaphysical works of the celebrated Immanuel Kant,* tr. John Richardson (London: W. Simpkin & R. Marshall, 1836), 118.
2 ____, *The Critique of Pure Reason,* tr. J.M.D. Meiklejohn (Radford, VA: Wilder Publications, 2008), 451.
3 Ibid., 67.
4 Anselm, *Proslogion,* tr. Thomas Williams (Indianapolis: Hackett Publishing Company Inc., 2001) chs. 2 and 3.
5 Kant, *Critique of Judgment¸* (New York: Cosimo Inc. 2007), 74.
6 ____, *The Critique of Practical Reason,* tr. Thomas Kingsmill Abbott (New York: Barnes & Noble Publishing, 2004), Book I, Ch. II.
7 ____, *Lectures on Ethics,* tr. L. Infield (London: Methuen, 1979), 99.
8 ____, *Opus postumum,* ed. Eckart Förster, tr. Eckart Förster and Michael Rosen, (Cambridge: Cambridge University Press, 1993), 198.
9 *Notes and Fragments: The Cambridge Edition of the Works of*

Immanuel Kant, (New York: Cambridge University Press, 2005), 404.

10 Kant, *The Critique of Practical Reason*, Book II, Ch. II.

11 ____, *The Conflict of the Faculties*, tr. Mary J. Gregor (New York: Abaris Books, 1992), 17.

12 Husserl, "Correspondence to Arnold Metzger" in *Husserl: Shorter Works*, ed. Peter McCormick and Frederick Elliston, (Notre Dame, Indiana: University of Notre Dame Press, 1981), 360.

13 Husserl's complete theory about how humans create meaning involves highly technical arguments that are beyond the scope of this book. For a comprehensive treatment of his thought, see David Carr, *The Paradox of Subjectivity: The Self in the Transcendental Tradition*, (New York: Oxford University Press, 1999).

14 Husserl, *The Crisis of European Sciences and Transcendental Phenomenology*, tr. D. Carr, (Evanston, Illinois: Northwestern University Press, 1970), 66.

15 Angela Ales Bello, *The Divine in Husserl and Other Explorations*, Analecta Husserliana, Vol. XCVIII, (Dordrecht: Springer, 2009), 53.

16 Husserl, Ms F I 22, 24.

17 ______, Ms F I 14, 43.

18 Angela Ales Bello, (2009), 66.

19 Husserl, Ms A V 21, 42a, cited in James G. Hart, "A Précis of an Husserlian Philosophical Theology," in *Essays in Phenomenological Theology*, ed. Steven W. Laycock and James G. Hart, (Albany: SUNY, 1986), 158.

20 ______, Ms A V 22, 46.

21 R.A. Mall, "The God of phenomenology in comparative contrast to that of philosophy and Theology," *Husserl Studies* Vol. 8 (1991): 10.

22 Husserl, Ms E III 9, 22a–22b, cited in James G. Hart, "Michel Henry's Phenomenological Theology of Life," *Husserl*

Studies, Vol. 15, No. 2 (October 1998): 211.

23 _____, Hua XXVII, 122, cited in James G. Hart, *The Person and the Common Life* (Dordrecht: Kluwer, 1992), 15–16.

24 _____, Ms. A V 21, 24b–25a.

25 Nietzsche, *Beyond Good & Evil*, tr. M. Faber, (Oxford: Oxford University Press, 1998), 43.

26 ______, *The Gay Science*, ed. Bernard Williams, (Cambridge: Cambridge University Press, 2003), 213.

27 ______, *The Twilight of the Idols and The Antichrist*, tr. Thomas Common, (Digireads.com Publishing 2009), 78.

28 ______, *On the Genealogy of Morals*, tr. Walter Kaufmann and R. J. Hollingdale, (New York: Random House, 1967), Essay II, 22.

29 ______, *On the Genealogy of Morals*, tr. Carol Diethe, (Cambridge: Cambridge University Press, 1994), 52.

30 ______, *Human, All Too Human*, tr. Gary Handwerk (Stanford: Stanford University Press, 1997), 107.

31 ______, "Morality as Anti-Nature," in *Twilight of the Idols*, (New York: Oxford University Press, 1998), Section 3.

32 Ibid., 20.

33 Nietzsche, *The Antichrist*, cited in *The Portable Nietzsche*, ed. and trans. Walter Kaufman, (New York: Penguin Books, 1954), 605ff.

34 _______, *The Gay Science*, 199. Nietzsche describes this situation as the "death" of God.

35 _______, *Thus Spoke Zarathustra*, ed. Adrian Del Caro and Robert Pippin, (Cambridge: Cambridge University Press, 2006), 206.

36 ______, "To the Unknown God," cited in Bruce Ellis Benson, *Pious Nietzsche: Decadence and Dionysian Faith*, (Bloomington: Indiana University Press, 2008), 22.

Chapter 3

The Leap of Faith

The possibility that we can acquire knowledge through reason or the senses is rejected by two noteworthy thinkers who, rather than adopting a skeptical position, claim that our lack of knowledge can point us to genuine belief in God. They outline the steps we should take when we recognise the limitations of human thought processes.

Making a bet

The seventeenth-century French philosopher Blaise Pascal introduced a new approach to the question of whether or not God exists. Pascal considered the world of his day to have become meaningless. He believed that the universe as studied by science is indifferent to the human condition, and provides no answers to our deepest longings. As a consequence, we are alienated and alone, lacking any understanding of the purpose of the world, and confused by the complexities of our own existence. Although we have the capacity to reason and are in that sense above nature, we can easily be destroyed by natural forces. We usually cope with this state of affairs by being constantly distracted, going from one excitement to another in the hope of finding something that is both good and lasting.

Pascal was a devout believer, and he undertook to persuade others of the value of belief in God, as understood in the Christian faith. One of the issues he addresses is the basis on which it is worthwhile to hold such a belief. He proposes that God is beyond anything we can comprehend, and we are therefore not in a position to produce evidence for his existence. On the other hand, we cannot prove that he does not exist. In these circumstances, neither the theist nor the atheist has any advantage over the other. Avoiding a choice, according to Pascal, amounts to deciding against belief in God, since it is only through exercising such a belief that the benefits of that decision can be obtained.

Christianity teaches that those who believe in God as revealed in Jesus Christ will have happiness in this life, and an infinity of happiness in the life to come. Those who do not believe will suffer eternal punishment in Hell. In view of these facts, Pascal argues that the most prudent thing for a nonbeliever to do is to weigh up the odds as to which will be the most beneficial—a life of believing in God and following his ways, or one of refusing to believe. This choice is presented in terms of making a wager, or a bet, that is based solely on self-interest.[1]

The basis of Pascal's argument is that if God exists, the benefits in this world of a relationship with him outweigh any benefits that could be claimed for a life of non-belief. Even if it should turn out that there is no God, Pascal reasons that the believer would still gain, since a life of devotion to the highest and best will always be more rewarding than one lived for selfish purposes. The desirability of making such a choice is indicated in the claim that there is an "infinite abyss" in the heart of every person that can only be filled by God himself.[2] Pascal describes the dedicated believer as faithful, honest, humble, grateful, generous, a sincere friend, and truthful. He thereby endorses the traditional view that the moral and spiritual transformation resulting from belief is unobtainable from any other source.

According to Pascal, there are only two possible positions on religious questions that human beings can adopt: belief in Christianity or the rejection of that faith. This claim dismisses all the other belief systems that have been spiritually life-sustaining for millions of people throughout history. Although Pascal does not directly refer to other religions in his discussion of the wager, he writes in other passages that without Jesus Christ, people who claim to know God and to demonstrate his existence can offer merely futile proofs for their faith.[3]

With regard to the wager and its effects on the eternal destiny of the individual, Pascal's rejection of other faiths means he has no interest in the way a relevant doctrine such as that of Hell is discussed outside a Christian context. Within the Quran, Hell is portrayed in perhaps an even more gruesome way than it appears in the Christian scriptures. It is the place where those who reject Islam will be sent. (Judaism does not have any doctrine of Hell in relation to eternal punishment.) If both of these sacred texts were to be compared, people faced with the choice of escaping either the Christian or the Quranic Hell would surely seek to avoid the latter. For Pascal's reasoning to hold, he would have to explain how the Christian concepts of Heaven and Hell are real, whereas their equivalents in Islamic teaching are invalid.

On the basis of Pascal's reasoning, if a skeptical person decides to believe in God, the form of such belief would lack the normal criteria for acceptance of its truth claims. The making of a decision that something is true, in full knowledge that the necessary evidence is lacking, would mean that beliefs of any kind could be acquired, regardless of their truth or falsity.[4] In acknowledging that it is impossible for people to change beliefs simply by an act of will, Pascal proposes a remedy for the person who may have a desire to believe, perhaps as a result of considering the wager. Such an individual, he suggests, should act as though belief were already present. This would involve engaging in religious practices such as attending masses, admitting moral failings, seeking divine grace, and submitting to the authority of God.[5] These habits of faith would then quieten any lingering intellectual doubt. Drawing on the Christian teaching that faith is a gift of God, Pascal asserts that God assists those who genuinely desire to believe, and who take action on the basis of that desire. Such people will be rewarded by having their initial faith confirmed, so that they then become rationally convinced of the truth of their belief.

Underlying Pascal's theory is the doctrine of God's ultimate incomprehensibility as taught in the scriptures. Since our capacity to reason is said to be inadequate, reliance is placed on the validating conviction that we are supposed to experience when we put into practice the required disciplines. But Pascal is then faced with the problem of accounting for the absence of conviction experienced by certain people whose behavior is consistent with the method he outlines. Pascal belonged to a movement within Catholicism which taught that those who have an explicit faith in Jesus Christ have already been chosen by God for salvation; everyone else is outside God's grace. (This doctrine is also embraced by some non-Catholic branches of Christianity.) Individuals who are unable to experience the conviction Pascal describes would therefore be seen as outside the group who have been granted the gift of faith. Similarly, Pascal states that it is necessary for a person to feel guilty and deserving of God's punishment. In his view, anyone who lacks these feelings has no genuine desire to believe. Yet that absence of desire, from Pascal's perspective, would be an indication that the individual concerned was not included within the ones originally chosen by God. Historically this doctrine has caused moral outrage, not only among the opponents of Christianity, but also within the community of believers.

Prior to the modern age and the significance it places on the role of the individual, people would probably have had less difficulty in accepting doctrines that were not confirmed by their own experiences. Even today, a view held by many Christian believers is that a lack of the sense of the presence of God is an unreliable indicator of his actual indwelling, or even the truth of his existence. It is possible, however, for a believer to be oppressed with the feeling of an inner division, where wholehearted commitment to the faith exists alongside a sense of failure caused by an absence of the kinds of experiences that are described in the scriptures as being evidence of divine presence.

With regard to people who endure this kind of inner turmoil, it would not be plausible for Pascal to claim that the desire to believe was lacking. On the basis of his reasoning, there would be no remaining category in which these individuals could be placed, other than among the group who will be rejected by God.

A consequence of Pascal's position is that if a person decides to engage in religious practices in the hope that she will become a believer, despite the fact that everything in her being points against the adoption of such a position, she is effectively saying to herself: "In the unlikely event that there is a God, I will follow these practices, just to be on the safe side." According to Pascal, such a calculated approach can lead to genuine faith, but it seems contrary to the biblical description of the attitude required in order for a relationship with God to be established, including the sense of guilt that Pascal describes elsewhere. A self-serving bet seems far removed from the act of asking God for mercy.

It has been argued that the greatest being we could conceive of would be less interested in the facts and doctrines we happen to embrace than in the qualities of character we develop.[6] Such a being would be unlikely to punish people simply because their beliefs were in error. The reason for individuals holding incorrect beliefs could reflect circumstances in their lives such as the kind of exposure, if any, they have had to Christian teachings, whether at a personal or a cultural level, and the extent to which their basic disposition and intellectual competence may problematize or even prohibit an engagement with a theistic position. In any case, Pascal cannot demonstrate: (a) that an individual's life beyond death is real and that it may last forever; (b) that life beyond death (if it does occur) involves only two possible states: absolute bliss or unspeakable horror; (c) that if there is a God, he is the kind of being who would determine the fate of individuals for eternity on the grounds that their beliefs were inaccurate during their limited period of time on this earth.

Pascal argues that if God exists, believers are better off than others, even in this world. Such a theory can be challenged on the grounds that theists are not necessarily more fulfilled than nontheists. The numerous strands of doctrine contained within Christian teachings can give rise to an enormous variety of personal experiences, some positive and some negative. Furthermore, Pascal has no way of showing that Christian believers have a more enriching life than those who embrace Judaism, Islam, or any other faith. Similarly with regard to the qualities displayed in the lives of believers, the history of the monotheisms shows no obvious differences between their adherents in terms of the virtues they develop. Each contains individuals who rise to the highest and those who sink to the lowest. This is the case with people of all cultures, regardless of whether or not they happen to accept the idea of a divine being. Such a reality undermines Pascal's views that Christian believers will always be in a better position than others, even if God does not exist, and that the process of transformation can only occur when Pascal's particular belief system is adopted.

The Absurd

In a Christian context, the question of belief in God is linked to the identity of the man Jesus. After his death and what was claimed to be his resurrection and ascension into Heaven, his followers divided into various groups who had differing views as to who he really was. Some regarded him as God and not truly man; some said he was the noblest of all created beings but not truly God. Others followed what became the orthodox view, established at special Councils in the fourth and fifth centuries. These declared that Jesus was equally man and God.

The nineteenth-century Danish philosopher Soren Kierkegaard originally held to the traditional view, but he became so disillusioned with the Christian church of his day that he developed a different way of approaching what he called the question of the "God-man."[7] He begins by suggesting that there exists an unknown X, to which he gives the name "God." Whether or not such a being exists can never be proved, since in Kierkegaard's view, any attempt to do so would require the prior assumption that he does, in fact, exist. Kierkegaard further claims that whatever we may imagine this divine being to be like, he is beyond our capacity to categorize or describe. Our reasoning capacities, which at most can give us probability, are inadequate to grasp the concept of God. He is the "absolutely different," which means that the kind of difference he has from us is infinitely greater than any other kind of difference.

According to Kierkegaard, if there is a God, it is necessary that we discover the truth about him, and what he requires of us. The difficulty we face is that the only ability we can apply when examining these issues is our limited reason. The doctrine that Jesus was fully God and fully man is described by Kierkegaard as offensive to our rational minds. Whereas God is said to be eternal (he has always existed and will always exist), Jesus was born into human history, grew into manhood and died. Also God is regarded as all-knowing and all-powerful, in contrast to Jesus, who had to learn things in the same way as any other child, and who suffered normal human conditions such as hunger and thirst. A further contrast is that while we cannot even know that God exists, the people of Jesus' time knew him as a member of a particular family. Because of the limitations of our reasoning processes, Kierkegaard argues that any theory about ultimate reality will take the form of a paradox, something that appears to our minds to be self-contradictory. Jesus is said to have had attributes of God and attributes of a man. Yet from a human viewpoint, it would be impossible for this combination to exist within a given individual. The dual nature of Jesus, which Kierkegaard calls the "Absolute Paradox," involves the greatest possible contradiction.[8] In respect of any other kind of paradox, we may attempt to resolve it, but the concept of the God-man takes us beyond the bounds of rational thought. From a human perspective it is an "absurdity."

Kierkegaard regards God as a subject to whom we can relate, rather than a concept that can be analyzed. It is only through a passionate commitment to the Absolute Paradox that we can experience the reality of God in our lives. Because the subject of our commitment is in conflict with our reason, when we submit ourselves to God, we are taking a risk that what we believe may not be objectively true. This risk-taking kind of faith is essential, since it takes us away from a false security based on the facts that both reason and revelation seek to establish. Kierkegaard rejects a commonly-accepted view that a person can weigh the evidence about Jesus and then decide to exercise faith in him. His position is that our defective reasoning processes conflict with the fundamental need we have to experience God by abandoning all sense of security.

Although Kierkegaard dismisses any reliance on the factual, which would include the truths contained in the biblical documents, his own writing presupposes the actual existence of God in the various claims he makes that God is a being who acts in a certain way, that we have turned against him, and that he can perform a miracle within us by giving us faith. The existence of God is also assumed in the description of the God-man. Kierkegaard describes what we experience when we take the risk of trusting in the Absolute Paradox, but he overlooks the fact that the idea of the God-man can only be obtained from the sacred texts. Similarly, Kierkegaard's theory is dependent on the biblical records in respect of the events of Jesus' life, death and resurrection, and for the idea that in our natural state we are estranged from God. Jesus' trust in the Hebrew scriptures, together with their descriptions of God's miraculous interventions in history, contrasts with Kierkegaard's claim that there is no ultimate value in accepting the truth of the biblical documents, even if they were shown as being completely reliable.

From the outset Kierkegaard presents a series of ideas that require the exercise of reason. Then he suggests that when we come to understand that reason has its limits, what we must accept is the absurd. But if we are to rely on reason to show us the limitations of reason, we would have to rely on reason to be convinced that there must be some kind of truth beyond reason. Whatever this truth may be, we cannot simply suspend reason in order to arrive at it. In seeking to motivate his readers to exercise faith, Kierkegaard is either appealing to their sense of reason (which would contradict his fundamental position) or he is appealing to their irrational side. An appeal to the irrational, however, cannot be made by the presentation of arguments, as Kierkegaard does in providing reasons for taking the leap of faith. Whenever we decide to take a risk, we have to be convinced that the risk is worth taking. The process of evaluating the benefit of the risk, as opposed to the benefit of not taking the risk, itself involves the exercise of reason. Although Kierkegaard rejects the idea of weighing the evidence and coming to a decision regarding the God-man, he is engaging in a similar kind of procedure by presenting the advantages of his own case. He argues that faith in the Absolute Paradox reinstates our relationship with God, giving us the conviction that what we believe has its own kind of truth, and that it is this risk-taking commitment through which our lives become meaningful.

An assumption made by Kierkegaard is that the idea of the God-man would be regarded by any rational person as absurd. Yet for the many people throughout history who have believed the ultimate miracle—that God created the universe out of nothing, the idea of God revealing himself in the form of a human being would seem to be no more difficult to accept; in fact, the doctrine of the Incarnation has been a fundamental belief from the time of the early church Councils, and it is usually placed in the category of mystery rather than absurdity. Kierkegaard would maintain, however, that people who examine the life and teachings of Jesus, and on that basis decide to exercise faith in his transforming power, would be rejected by God. The position held by Kierkegaard would commit him to the view that even if such people accepted the paradox of the God-man, they would not be engaging in the necessary kind of risk-taking that involves exercising faith in the absurd.

The importance of reason is evident in the cases of people who have maintained intellectual objections to the Christian message for most of their lives, but in the end have come to the conclusion that it is true, and have then exercised the kind of faith that is required. (Such a situation can of course occur with an individual who embraces any other belief system.) It does not necessarily require the exercise of faith in order to believe that Jesus was God incarnate. A person could come to believe in the truth of Christianity based on the recorded evidence—in particular, the transformation in the lives of the early disciples following Jesus' resurrection from the dead. Accepting that these events occurred, however, need not lead an individual to the kind of risk-taking personal commitment that in Kierkegaard's view is essential. Faith in the Absolute Paradox does not occur in an intellectual vacuum, even if it could be shown that the process is entirely the work of God. Overall, Kierkegaard's belief in what he calls the Absurd could not exist in the absence of historical revelation, nor can it be completely independent from the exercise of reason. On those grounds, Kierkegaard is unable to substantiate his view that the taking of a risk in the unknowable is a prerequisite to the experience of God.

Summary

Whereas most of the thinkers discussed earlier place some value on our reasoning capacities, or in addition, on their personal experience of God, Pascal and Kierkegaard share the view that his existence is a mystery. But the remedies they propose for our lack of knowledge point in opposite directions. Pascal suggests that people should, in effect, rely on reason in weighing the benefits, in relation to both the here and the hereafter, of making the decision to believe. Kierkegaard on the other hand describes Christian belief as absurd. Yet he advocates making the irrational choice to believe in Jesus as the God-man, while at the same time taking the risk that God may not even exist.

The thinkers we have examined up to this point have a generally agreed definition of a divine being. Some of the philosophers who followed challenge the idea that a particular concept can ever be defined, but that all meaning is dependent on the contribution that we ourselves make.

1 Pascal, *Pensées*, (New York: Start Publishing LLC, 2012), para 233.
2 _____, *Pensées*, (New York; Penguin Books, 1966), 75.
3 _____, *Pensées*, (New York: Penguin, 1985), 189.
4 Bernard Williams, "Deciding to believe" in *Problems of the Self*, (New York: Cambridge, 1973), 148.
5 Pascal, *Pensées*, (2012), para 233.
6 Gregory Mougin and Elliott Sober, "Betting Against Pascal's Wager," *Noûs*, 28, 3 (1994), footnote 8, 394.
7 Kierkegaard, *Sickness unto Death*, (Radford VA: A & D Publishing, 2008), 105.
8 *Søren Kierkegaard's Journals and Papers*, ed. and tr. Howard and Edna Hong (Bloomington, Indiana: Indiana University Press, 1967–1978), Vol. 3, 402 (IV B 75).

Chapter 4

Beyond Revealed Truth

The period from the seventeenth century to the middle of the twentieth century is known as the age of modernity. It arose in part from the decline of the social institutions and the religious world view that had predominated in the Middle Ages. Among the consequences were a reduction in the previous sense of certainty, and the emergence of a new kind of belief that human beings could control their own destiny, both in terms of creating values for themselves, and in achieving mastery over the forces of nature.

In Western thought today, modernity has largely given way to postmodernity, which is characterised by the lack of belief in absolute truth. Reality is not something "out there" to which we have access, but merely that which we construct in our minds. The effect of these ideas is to reduce truth to the merely relative. Within postmodern philosophy and theology, the notion of God as a particular being who possesses a set of attributes, is regarded as inappropriate in the attempt to comprehend the divine. Instead, scholars committed to theism write of a concept beyond our powers of language to describe.

Recent approaches to the question of God have included a renewed interest in the experiences of mysticism, and in the extent to which they may shed light on the meaning of our existence. Mystical practices have been known in most cultures throughout history, but one of the difficulties in determining whether they can provide any form of knowledge lies in understanding the nature of the experiences themselves. They are generally regarded as altered states of consciousness, and may consist of an immediate awareness that reality is one.[1] In this state, described as "non-dual awareness," individual things seem to lose their independent existence as everything is absorbed into the whole. There is no longer a subject or object of experience as personal identity is dissolved into the greater unity.[2] Entry into this state requires that the mind be completely stilled and detached from all objects of desire. Mystics recount a cessation of reasoning functions and sensory capacity in a feeling of timelessness and spacelessness. They also describe a sense of peace and bliss in the loss of their identifiable selves to this nameless mystery. The state is likened to being "in a vast and profound solitude, to which no created thing has access, in an immense and boundless desert."[3]

Characteristics of the above form of mystical experience include a feeling of the sacred that seems to transcend ordinary concerns in pointing towards ultimate reality and truth. For the duration of the events, mystics are aware of continuing consciousness, but their experiences cannot be reduced to language or to the kind of descriptions that would occur in normal communication. On the other hand, certain feelings of the events are retained that enable comparisons to be drawn between the accounts given in different cultural contexts.

Within the monotheisms there have always been individuals, and in some cases groups of people, who claim to have had mystical experiences of various kinds. Religions have then had to determine the extent, if any, to which these experiences can be incorporated into orthodox doctrines. Mystics have at times been regarded as possessing special insights into truth, and the material they present has been used to reinforce the teachings of the particular tradition. On other occasions their ideas have been seen as dangerous or subversive.[4] Among mystics themselves is a division between those who desire to be absorbed into a unity with God or the ultimate mystery, and those who believe a gulf exists between human beings and their Creator, and who seek merely a form of intimate relationship with him. These different approaches reflect the alternative views that God is inseparable from the individual, or that he is transcendent to the whole of creation.

Certain accounts given by mystics in the medieval period involve the desire to be united with Christ, together with a recognition that the individual can never be identical with the divine. Catherine of Siena was said to have undergone states of penance from a young age, praying almost continually, fasting, and sleeping little.[5] In her twenties she claims to have celebrated a mystical marriage to Christ. A further example is Teresa of Ávila, who had a range of experiences including a loss of personal identity, mental functioning and sensory capacities. She ultimately attained what she believed was a spiritual union with Christ, which she describes in terms of sexual intimacy.[6]

With regard to experiences of non-dual awareness, reports given by mystics from various backgrounds suggest that there is a definable common core in these states, separating them from any associated interpretations, and that this form of mystical experience is universal.[7] It would follow therefore that if a theist were to interpret the encounter as indicating a special kind of relationship with God, that belief would represent merely an overlay to the experience itself. Since we normally trust the reliability of our senses and our reasoning processes to give us access to the physical world, should we discover that the mind can function in a way that transcends the limitations of our normal functioning, it is reasonable to conclude that what is experienced in these altered states of consciousness indicates the existence of a different dimension of reality that can be accessed independently of any belief system.

A contrasting view in relation to the commonalities of mysticism is taken by those who claim that there can be no experience that is beyond the abilities of humans to describe. An object of experience is always distinguishable in our minds from other objects, so that a mystical experience should be analyzable in the same way as any other. Whereas defenders of the commonality position draw a distinction between the mystical state itself and interpretations that may be attempted after the event, their opponents argue that every kind of experience we have is affected by our cultural and language backgrounds, and that the nature of an experience is itself determined by these factors. The commonality advocates respond that the unusual qualities of the mystical state mean it is unlike any other experience imaginable, and that it cannot be subjected to an analysis involving language and concepts. They also argue that if our understanding were in fact governed by cultural factors, we would expect that the experience itself would merely confirm our existing beliefs. No explanation could then be advanced as to the reason mystics of all persuasions present similar kinds of accounts.

The mystical state is generally reached through a progression of stages based on meditative practices, where the individual focuses on a particular concept or object until extraneous matters recede into the background and ultimately disappear. It has been argued that if God is the focus of the earlier stages, a union with the divine must also apply in respect of the final stage. The proponents of this view claim that even when a non-dual state of awareness is reached where no kind of identification is possible, God is necessarily involved in the total process. By contrast, supporters of the commonality position regard the loss of all forms of identity as pointing towards the existence of a dimension that is irreducible to the concept of a particular being, regardless of the method used to reach that state.

The two examples of medieval mystics discussed above could suggest that the divine is mysteriously accessible in these kinds of encounters. If this were the case, however, there would be no explanation for the significant differences in the interpretation of such experiences recounted by individuals of various religious persuasions. For example, a Jewish or Muslim mystic's experience would not involve a marriage to Christ.

Differences of this kind are in sharp contrast to the similarities that exist in the states of union described by mystics from the various traditions where all awareness of the self disappears. In the kind of experience involving a "mystical marriage," the individual identity of both partners would be preserved. The Christian scriptures describe such a marriage between Christ and the church, his bride, where the separate identity of the two is carried over into the heavenly sphere.[8] Any experience based on a distinction between the mystic and the divine would be merely an exalted form of the bond that is said to exist between God and the believer.

The study of mysticism has historically been associated with a set of ideas defined within Christianity as "negative theology." Its equivalents can be found in Judaism and Islam. A feature of this approach is the claim that human beings can have a deep-seated desire for something they cannot identify. This may involve a feeling that the realization of such a desire would bring a greater fulfillment than anything we can experience in the present world, including conventional faith in the God portrayed in scripture.[9] A relationship with this unnameable divinity is thought to be our ultimate spiritual destiny.

In seeking to move beyond the idea of an all-powerful Creator, negative theologians propose that God can only be discussed in terms of what he is not. Traditionally he has been portrayed as the greatest concept our minds can imagine, but at the same time he is described as a being who, like us, can think, feel, act, and enter into relationships. The extent to which God's existence can be compared with our own is a subject that has engaged philosophers and theologians throughout the history of the monotheisms.

A problem faced in discussing God is that we either attribute qualities to him such as goodness and justice that can have meaning only on the basis of our own understanding and experience of these qualities, or else we refrain from describing him at all, in which case a relationship with him would seem impossible. The fear has been expressed that if we adopt the former approach, we risk creating a divinity confined to our limited human concepts, or even using assumptions regarding his character for the purposes of achieving our own ends. With regard to the idea that our lack of knowledge precludes the possibility of a relationship with God at all, negative theologians describe the mystery in ways that in their view enable such a possibility to be realized.

In the thought of the sixth-century Christian writer Dionysius, God is beyond concepts such as being and non-being, time and eternity; he is unknowable because he exceeds the idea of a being who exists. Dionysius also proposes that the difference between God and his creatures is so great that it transcends both similarity and difference.[10] He describes it as being prior to distinctions and to the absence of distinctions, a negation of negation and a negation of affirmation, beyond assertion and beyond denial. In the "brilliant darkness" of God, however, Dionysius claims we can achieve a union with the divine and a form of knowledge that emerges from a state of unknowing.[11]

The problem of connecting with something we cannot describe or even imagine is addressed several centuries later by the medieval mystic Meister Eckhart. His solution is to suggest that there are two forms of God. One can be spoken of and addressed in prayer, as occurs in traditional teaching and practice. The other he defines as the "Godhead" or the "God beyond God," which is a mystery that falls outside humans' power to conceptualize.[12] From Eckhart's perspective, the Godhead is so far removed from us that even to describe it in superlative terms would be to commit an act of injustice. In order to experience a relationship with this mystery, we must remove from our awareness the qualities and characteristics that are normally attributable to God. We are then able to enter into the kind of state that has been described by mystics throughout history.

Although both the experiences of negative theologians and the mystical states transcending identity awareness have been linked to the idea of the divine, their content lacks the distinctive features of the all-powerful being depicted in the scriptures who intervenes in history and who loves and cares for his creatures. The theories of negative theologians are generally not accepted by mainstream thinkers within the faith traditions, but they are the subject of intense interest among philosophers and those theologians who are seeking new ways of contemplating the infinite.

1 W. T. Stace, *Mysticism and Philosophy* (London: Macmillan, 1960), 78.
2 It has been claimed that the capacity for this kind of experience is evidence of a neurological dysfunction. This question will be discussed in Chapter 11.
3 William James, *The Varieties of Religious Experience: A Study in Human Nature,* (New York: Longmans, Green, and Co., 1902), 407.
4 Don Cupitt, *Mysticism after Modernity,* (Oxford: Blackwell, 1998), 3–4.
5 Karen Scott, "St. Catherine of Siena, 'Apostola,'" *Church History,* 61, 1 (1992), 35.
6 Judith S. Neaman, "Potentiation, Elevation, Acceleration: Prerogatives of Women Mystics," *Mystics Quarterly,* Vol. 14, No. 1 (March 988), pp. 22–31.
7 W. T. Stace, op. cit., 11.
8 See Revelation 21: 2.
9 Adriaan T. Peperzak, "Affective Theology, Theological Affectivity," in Jeffrey Bloechl (ed.), *Religious Experience and the End of Metaphysics* (Bloomington: Indiana University Press, 2003), 94–105.
10 Denys Turner, "Tradition and Faith," *International Journal of*

Systematic Theology, Vol. 6, No. 1, (2004): 26.

11 __________, *The Darkness of God: Negativity in Christian Mysticism*, (Cambridge: Cambridge University Press, 1995), 21.

12 J. M. Clark, *Meister Eckhart*, (London: Nelson & Sons, 1957), 183.

Chapter 5

God as Mystery

The two philosophers discussed in this chapter, Derrida and Marion, are interested in the question of negative theology, though they depart from it in different ways. The former challenges its attempts to transcend language, while the latter situates his thinking beyond both positive and negative approaches to the question of whether God can be described by finite beings.

What is God?

A central concern of the French philosopher Jacques Derrida is the way language is structured, and in his later work he applies his theory of language in examining the claims of negative theology. Derrida's theory seeks to undermine the traditional assumption that there is a direct connection between words and the objects or concepts to which they refer, such as the word "house" indicating a building where people live. In Derrida's view by contrast, the meaning of a word is not primarily related to some object as defined by its accepted use within a given culture, but is a consequence of its difference from all other words.[1] The latter in turn have their own system of differences, the result being the formation of an endless chain. Furthermore, the contexts in which the terms are used will affect the way they are understood. Words, together with individual beings and things, are continually modified by shifting backgrounds of difference and changing contexts. It is for this reason that there are no absolute or self-contained meanings.

Derrida suggests that difference in its original sense is not really a word or a concept, and that as an endless process of contrasts, it cannot even be said to exist. Parallels have been drawn between this theory and negative theology, which discusses God as a mystery beyond the powers of language to describe. While admitting that in certain respects the two theories are similar, Derrida draws attention to the areas where they differ, and he outlines the problems he finds in negative theology's attitude to language. His basic argument is that although negative theologians claim they are portraying something we can never grasp, they cannot avoid forming some kind of positive conception of God—in particular, the idea that he is a being with certain attributes. In Derrida's view, we cannot use words to describe something that is said to exist beyond the realm of language.[2] Even if God is not regarded as an individual being, that in itself would not imply that "beyond being" equals "beyond language." Whatever God may be, once we start thinking about him, we are using words and concepts.

In order to say what God is not, according to Derrida, we would have to list all the characteristics traditionally attributed to him. If we claim that he is none of these, we are placing a limit on what he could actually be. Furthermore, if God is the ultimate mystery, we would have no way of knowing whether he may actually incorporate some or all of the features on our list. In practice, Derrida argues, descriptive terms such as "being," "love," "goodness," while being denied to God, are then re-ascribed to him at a higher level.

The negative theologian Dionysius writes about the immediacy of a presence, which he describes as a genuine vision and knowledge of God. For Derrida, such an encounter would indicate that a certain idea of God can, in fact, be expressed in words, thereby suggesting the existence of a particular being. Yet Dionysius proposes that because speech can never convey the experience of God's presence, we should remain silent. In Derrida's view, this represents an admission that there exists an actual being whom our words are inadequate to describe. Such an interpretation is reinforced by terms used in negative theology such as "truth" and "revelation," which imply that we can at least have some awareness of who God is. Dionysius describes awakening to the darkness of unknowing, which is both the unveiling of a mystery and the imparting of a secret. In Derrida's view, the possession of a secret means that it is expressible in language, and must therefore be categorized as knowledge.[3]

A further problem for Derrida is that negative theologians express a strong desire to experience union with God, but on the other hand, in order to support their view that the deity can never be the object of any human thought, they claim it is necessary to renounce any desire to experience or to conceptualize the divine. Similarly, these thinkers discuss acts such as praising God and offering prayers to him, which would imply that he not only exists, but that he is the kind of being who is worthy of such devotion. Eckhart writes that in order to experience the "imprint" of God, the soul or innermost being of the individual must be pure, and that the soul in such a state is one with God. Once again, this description in Derrida's thinking simply reinforces the idea that God is a particular kind of being.

Derrida rejects both the traditional Christian attempt to define what God is, and the negative theologians' position that something beyond our understanding gives rise to goodness and truth. In Derrida's view, it is impossible to make an absolute claim that there is something that could be called "God," or that there is a certain way this concept could be defined. The deepest needs of the individual, he claims, can never be satisfied by faith in a specific being. On the other hand, Derrida has a profound interest in the question of God, due to its history and also because of his own personal inclinations. The difficulty he faces is that his theory prevents him from attributing any name to what he regards as a mystery, since that approach would suggest the existence of a being possessing certain attributes.

Alongside his view that the concept of God may not have

any real meaning, Derrida recognises a deep longing in the human heart. This leads him to suggest that "God" is the name of what we most love and desire, even though we can never form a view as to what this could be. He refers to a question raised by the early Christian theologian and philosopher Bishop Augustine, "What do I love when I love my God?"[4] Augustine's considered response is that the life of faith is one of endless seeking, whereas for Derrida, the question has no answer. Having admitted that he could pass for an atheist, Derrida makes the surprising statement that he has prayed to God all his life, and that he takes God as his witness. He is confident that the ultimate unknowable mystery is aware of his struggles, but at the same time he wonders why he even addresses a God of whom he knows nothing. Derrida also has a sense that God knows what it is like to have a son who is lacking in love, which is presumably a reference to his own inability to form a view of God that would enable a relationship with him to be established. Then after describing himself as being prone to tearfulness, he suggests that this form of self-expression could be God weeping within him.[5]

The longing for what is understood as God, Derrida claims, cannot ultimately be decided in favor of theism or atheism—in fact he claims that certain forms of atheism involve the most intense desire for God.[6] Although Derrida rejects negative theology, and he does not embrace any form of traditional theism, he has a deep interest in the concept of the Messiah. Within Jewish thought, this term refers to a promised leader or king who will deliver his people from bondage and usher in an age of peace. Centuries later, Christianity designated Jesus of Nazareth as having fulfilled this prophecy. Islam accepts that Jesus was the Messiah, but Jews and Muslims do not endorse the Christian view that he was God in human form. Derrida questions the idea of an actual Messiah, while acknowledging the persuasiveness of this belief within the various religious traditions. He then suggests that the doctrine of the Messiah is indicative of an underlying and indeterminate "messianicity" that extends beyond its particular historical expressions. In Derrida's thought, the messianic appeal has a universal structure that is concerned with questions of salvation and fundamental justice.[7] It involves a sense of expectation and a commitment to the future.

Whereas much of religious teaching involves the acquiring of knowledge, Derrida advocates an experience that transcends the factual. The basis of this kind of experience he calls "faith," but unlike our normal understanding of the term, the faith outlined by Derrida is not directed to anything or anyone. Having defined messianicity as the promise of "something or someone to come,"[8] he suggests that we cannot know what or who will come, or even whether such an event will ever occur. Derrida's position is that if we believed in the eventual arrival of something or some being, we would already have formed a particular concept of it. No thing or being can be described in definitive terms, and we can never know whether an ultimate mystery even exists.

The unusual approach Derrida takes to this question is that rather than being distressed over our lack of knowledge, we should have a passion for what he calls "the impossible"—an experience of something unforeseen, where we have no certainty that anything at all will eventuate. This approach is contrasted with what Derrida calls "religion," which is based on the various historical revelations, and includes things such as doctrine, ethics, and ritual observances.

Derrida's writing faces problems in the way he discusses both faith and love. Religious faith is based on God's self-revelation in the scriptures, these texts providing reasons for the need to believe. From this it follows that there is something to which faith is to be directed, whereas the experience Derrida describes has no content and therefore seems to lack meaning.

Furthermore, unless the object of faith is identified, there is no basis on which it could be called "God," and there would no point in having faith in something that may never become real. Regarding the kind of love Derrida has for the unknowable mystery, he is unable to show that he is referring to something rather than to nothing, nor can he rule out the possibility that the unknown could even be a source of evil.

The attitude Derrida has to the question of God is complex. He desires to have a relationship with some kind of divine being, but his theory that there is no such thing as a fixed meaning prevents him from forming the conclusion that a being called God actually exists. On the other hand, Derrida's engagement with the ultimate mystery is of such intensity that it provokes a deep emotional response within him. It is as though a firm faith in God's existence would not result in the kind of experience that for Derrida seems to be the most meaningful, and for this reason he needs to leave the question in suspense.

God without being

Two of the thinkers discussed earlier, Immanuel Kant and Edmund Husserl, draw on particular kinds of inner experience to support their view that a God of some kind exists. Their respective positions also include the exercise of faith. A contemporary French philosopher, Jean-Luc Marion, uses everyday experiences as evidence for his theory that an unnameable God takes the initiative in acts of self-revelation, though faith does not have the kind of significance in his thought that it has for Kant and Husserl.

One of Marion's aims is to justify religion in the light of his own development of Husserl's philosophy, which examines human experience in the world as the basis of knowledge.[9] Marion sees a problem in the way philosophy as a whole has addressed the question of religion and religious experiences, in that it has either excluded religion from its domain of inquiry, or sought to impose its own criteria in matters of interpretation. In the former case, nothing meaningful can be said about the experiences of religion, while the latter attempt results in the loss of their specifically religious quality.[10] An associated problem concerns the way theology has been contaminated by philosophical approaches, an example being the idea that God is the explanation for everything that exists.

According to Marion, the nature of God cannot be understood through the many ways we may try to conceptualize him. However much we seek to imagine a being totally unlike ourselves, our attempts will always fail; the unlikeness between ourselves and God is of such a magnitude that it transcends our thought processes as finite beings. Even the most fundamental of all distinctions—that between what is and what is not—becomes insignificant when compared with the absolute difference between God and his creatures.[11] Making statements about God raises so many problems that in Marion's view, "One must obtain forgiveness for every essay in theology," the reason being that "theology consists precisely in saying that for which only another can answer."[12]

The distance between ourselves and God is described by Marion as a "hyperbolic separation," so that we should think of God as "without being" or as a "supreme nonbeing."[13] This does not mean, however, that we can say, "God is not," but on the other hand it does not imply the medieval idea that God exists necessarily—that he must exist. It is because of our distance from God that he can reveal himself to us, and in this context, Marion outlines what he calls an unthinkable paradox: "[T]he intimacy of man with the divine *grows* with the gap that distinguishes them."[14] The basis of this portrayal is that when we conceive of God as a being, we make him too much like ourselves, and as a result, he is unable to reveal himself in all his mystery. God is rather to be experienced as a presence without limits, a "dazzling evidence"—of the kind that would not be possible in respect of any visible thing. Marion writes that God "shines by his absence."[15]

The idea that we can make no definitive statements about God has a similarity to the approach of negative theology, but Marion resists this comparison on the grounds that his idea of God is beyond both affirmation and negation. He argues that if human desires and beliefs cannot reveal God, their denial or contradiction will similarly be inadequate. In this context Marion quotes from a fourth-century church father: "God as such cannot be spoken. The perfect knowledge of God is so to know him that we are sure we must not be ignorant of Him, yet cannot describe Him."[16] If God's name is not silenced, he becomes a subject of our reason or our sense of morality, and is thereby denied his difference and distance from us. Marion goes so far as to say that we cannot have a "relation" to God, because as one of the poles of the relation, he remains in total indeterminacy.

In Marion's view, since the time of Descartes there has been a tendency for our experience of the world to be interpreted subjectively. By contrast, Marion describes the manner in which God's revelation of himself can so overwhelm or "bedazzle" us that our own manner of thinking becomes irrelevant. This situation contrasts with the traditional view that the only means whereby we can engage with a transcendent God is through faith. That kind of faith is considered by Marion to be the consequence of a belief that the infinite cannot be revealed within the finite sphere, so that faith becomes a compensation for the lack of a direct experience of God.[17] It is only the divine who can take the initiative in acts of self-giving, and the more indefinable he is, the more intimate is the communion he has with his creatures.

As discussed above, the view of the negative theologian Dionysius is questioned in Derrida's claim that Dionysius is assuming the existence of an exalted being who is beyond our capacity to describe. Marion contests this interpretation by suggesting that what is being referred to by Dionysius is not a particular being but "the One who de-nominates."[18] This approach is seen by Marion as being beyond a process of saying or unsaying, naming or un-naming, but instead marks God's absence, anonymity, and withdrawal.[19] It evokes the kind of praise that transcends the possibility of knowledge. For Derrida, praise inevitably involves the application of descriptive titles to God, and we can only praise something we have reason to believe is praiseworthy. Marion counters that rather than being a means of defining individuals, proper names are merely useful ways of referring to them. A distance is thereby maintained between ourselves and a God who is "anonymous and outside every name."[20] This anonymity can give rise to a multiplication of praises and names attributable to God, none of which can ever be adequate to define him.

Although the idea of God as an unnameable mystery involves paradoxes of description, Marion seeks to clarify his approach in his discussion of the icon. He draws a distinction between an icon and an idol, the significant difference between the two being the manner in which a given object is viewed. If it merely satisfies our gaze, it becomes an idol, the result of our own projection. It exhausts our aspirations and expectations and freezes them into an image that is nothing more than a mirror of ourselves. As Marion writes, "Name your idol, and you will know who you are."[21] A variety of things can become idols, including works of art and literature. Marion advances the view that arguments for and against the idea of God are in themselves idolatrous since they reduce God to a concept in our minds.

In contrast to the idol, an icon is not limited by the visible, but allows the visible to be overcome by the invisible. The icon "opens in a face that gazes at our gazes,"[22] offering an abyss that can never be fathomed. It shatters our previously held concepts, such as the idea of God as the supreme being, enabling us to resist the attempt to comprehend the incomprehensible, and to receive instead what the icon gives in the form of an excess. The effect of this givenness is such that the phenomenon of the icon can overwhelm and even crush the self. Marion identifies the ultimate example of the icon as Christ, who is described in the scriptures as "the image of the invisible God,"[23] whose presence can never be mastered by human gaze.

Marion belongs to a movement within philosophy begun by Husserl that examines the inner processes by which we give meaning to our existence. Such an approach is modified by Marion, who proposes a kind of "givenness" to some experiences that is not dependent on the conditions within an individual that enable experience to occur.[24] Marion uses examples such as love or a work of art that can take us by surprise and are beyond our ability to conceptualize. Because of the way they overwhelm us, they are defined as "saturated phenomena." Givenness is so fundamental to our existence that even ordinary things can be experienced in this way, depending on how they are viewed.

The idea of saturation is used by Marion in his discussion of Christian doctrines. At the celebration of the Eucharist (also known as Holy Communion), bread and wine are consecrated by the priest, by means of which they are believed to become the body and blood of Christ, though their basic attributes remain unchanged. Marion interprets the givenness of God in the sacrifice of Christ as an abandonment whereby the divine is given to the world: "The Eucharistic gift consists in the fact that in it love forms one body with our body."[25] Participation in this sacrament is an encounter with the divine that can take the form of a "stupor" or a "terror" imposed by the excess of its incomprehensibility.[26] The miracle of Jesus' resurrection is portrayed as a phenomenon "where the manifest given goes beyond not only what a human look can bear without being blinded and dying, but what the world in its essential finitude can receive and contain."[27]

Marion attempts to separate the nature of overwhelming experiences from the individual's existing beliefs, which traditionally have involved the exercise of faith, as revealed in historical events. The kind of faith Marion describes is a gift of God that "allows reception of the intelligence of the phenomenon and the strength to bear the glare of its brilliance."[28] What would be required, however, for an individual to identify a particular experience as being of God would be a prior belief in his existence, together with an assumption that only the divine could originate such an event.

In claiming that it requires faith to recognise God in the experience, Marion overlooks the fact that although faith is said to be given by God, it does not arise in a situation devoid of any supporting evidence. Marion is unable to establish that the experience of bedazzlement is a proof of God's self-givenness rather than being a deep response within the individual to what is already believed about God's saving work in Christ. The kind of faith that relies on historical evidence and the use of reason is dismissed by Marion as "philosophical," but the absence of such evidence could result in the experience being merely an inner emotional response to something unknown. For example, we may find ourselves overwhelmed by a work of art, but that experience could be attributable to our inner response to beauty rather than to a process of self-giving on the part of the work itself. Since we have the ability to respond at a deep level to that which inspires us, the only legitimate proposition that could be advanced in a religious context is that where God is already believed to exist, the kind of response Marion describes may be evoked in a celebration such as the Eucharist.

The faith Marion affirms is that relating to bedazzlement, so he needs to account for the situation of those who do not enjoy that experience. It would seem that many believers are not overcome by stupor or terror in their religious observances.

Nevertheless, such people would have faith in Jesus as the redeemer of the world, both as revealed in the scriptures and as taught by the church. According to Marion, this kind of faith lacks validity in that it is subsumed within a conventional philosophical outlook. He is therefore committed to one of two positions: a) that the people he refers to will be rejected by God because they lack an authentic faith, or b) that they are not receiving everything God has to offer in the experience of saturation. If Marion holds to the latter view, he would be conceding that ultimate acceptance by God is dependent on the kind of faith that has sustained believers throughout history, rather than on particular kinds of experience that may not be available to everyone.

Marion attempts to show that belief in God can be supported through an examination of the manner in which we can be overwhelmed in similar ways by both religious and everyday experiences. His theory offers no explanation as to the reason these experiences do not occur as a matter of course in a religious context, and he lacks a justification for the pronouncements he makes about the nature of God that are not contained in the scriptures or in the teachings of the church. The unusual and limited view of faith that he outlines runs counter to the typical experience of committed believers.

Summary

The link between Derrida and Marion is their rejection of the idea that God is a being who can be described as having certain characteristics and who is the cause of everything that exists. Both philosophers describe intense experiences that can be interpreted as originating in God, though Derrida's uncertainty about the existence of the divine contrasts with Marion's absolute conviction that God engages in overwhelming acts of self-revelation.

A further development in philosophical thought, which we

will now examine, involves the displacement of the concept of a divine being in favor of a mysterious source which gives rise to the existence of everything that is.

1 Derrida, "*Différance,*" in *Margins of Philosophy*, tr. Alan Bass (Chicago: University of Chicago Press, 1982), 11.
2 ______, "How to avoid speaking: Denials" in *Derrida and Negative Theology*, ed. Harold Coward and Toby Foshay, (Albany: State University of New York Press, 1992), 77 and 81.
3 Ibid., 94.
4 John D. Caputo, *The prayers and tears of Jacques Derrida: religion without religion*, (Bloomington: Indiana University Press, 1997), 334.
5 Geoffrey Bennington and Jacques Derrida, *Jacques Derrida*, tr. Geoffrey Bennington, (Chicago: University of Chicago Press, 1993), 224.
6 Derrida, *On the Name*, ed. and tr. Thomas Dutoit (Stanford: Stanford University Press, 1995), 80.
7 ______, *Specters of Marx*, tr. Peggy Kamuf, (Abingdon, Oxon: Routledge, 1994), 210.
8 ______, *Responsibilities of Deconstruction*, ed. Jonathon Dronsfield and Nick Midgley, (Coventry: University of Warwick, 1997), 3.
9 Marion, *The Visible and the Revealed*, tr. Christina M. Gschwandtner, (New York: Fordham University Press, 2008), 1.
10 Ibid., 18.
11 Marion, *God Without Being*, tr. Thomas A. Carlson (Chicago: University of Chicago Press, 1995), 88.
12 Ibid., 2.
13 Marion, *The Idol and Distance*, tr. Thomas A. Carlson, (New York: Fordham University Press, 2001), 138.
14 Ibid., 80.

15 Marion, "Metaphysics and Phenomenology: A Relief for Theology," tr. Thomas A. Carlson, *Critical Inquiry*, Vol. 20, 4, (1994), 589.

16 Hilary of Poitiers, *De Trinitate*, II, 7, PL 10, 36, *Nicene and Post-Nicene Fathers*, vol. 9, ed. Philip Schaff, (Grand Rapids, Mich.: Eerdmans, 1981), cited in Jean-Luc Marion, *In Excess: Studies of Saturated Phenomena*, tr. Robyn Horner and Vincent Berraud, (New York: Fordham University Press, 2002), 158.

17 Marion, "They recognized him; And he became invisible to them," *Modern Theology* 18, (2002): 145–146.

18 ______, *In Excess*, 140.

19 ______, "In the Name: How to Avoid Speaking of 'Negative Theology'" in *God, the Gift, and Postmodernism,* ed. John D. Caputo and Michael J. Scanlon, (Bloomington: Indiana University Press, 1999), 29.

20 Anselm K. Min, "Naming the Unnameable God: Levinas, Derrida, and Marion," *International Journal for Philosophy of Religion*, 60, 1/3, (2006): 108.

21 Marion, *In Excess*, 61.

22 ______, *God Without Being*, 19.

23 Colossians 1:15.

24 Marion, "The Banality of Saturation," tr. Jeffrey L. Kosky, in *Counter-Experiences*, ed. Kevin Hart, (Notre Dame, Indiana: University of Notre Dame Press, 2007), 401–402.

25 _______, *God Without Being,* 3–4.

26 _______, *In Excess,* 161.

27 _______, *Communio,* ed. J-L Marion and Hans Urs von Balthasar, cited in Emmanuel Falque, *"Larvatus pro Deo,"* tr. Robyn Horner, in *Counter-Experiences,* ed. Kevin Hart, (Notre Dame, Indiana: University of Notre Dame Press, 2007), 192.

28 Marion, "They recognized him; And he became invisible to them," 150.

Chapter 6

A Truth Beyond God

Challenges to the existence of a personal God have been proposed by two modern philosophers, Heidegger and Deleuze, who substitute for a divine act of creation the idea of an undifferentiated state of potential from which arises everything that exists. Their views contain certain similarities to a concept outlined by the Ancient Greek thinker Plato.

Belonging to being

The claim by Marion that theology has been too heavily influenced by traditional philosophy is shared by the twentieth-century philosopher Martin Heidegger, who similarly replaces the idea of God as the highest being with the concept of an unnameable mystery. But whereas Marion's focus is on the self-revelation of the deity, Heidegger considers all theological questions to be secondary to the focus of his work, which is the question of being.

Heidegger endorses the view proposed by Nietzsche that in the modern world, the idea of God has lost its meaning. All we now have, as a substitute for the divine, is a reliance on science and our own reason. In his later work Heidegger suggests that as a result of our dependence on the rational, we suffer from the absence of what he calls "the holy," defined as "the essential sphere of divinity."[1] This description does not refer to a being we could call "God"; it rather suggests a mystery that is always withdrawn from our understanding. If, however, we make the necessary preparation, including entry into a state of meditative stillness, we may one day be able to experience the holy. Although Heidegger began his life as a person of faith, it is doubtful that he retained a belief in the Judeo-Christian

God, since his concept of the holy is beyond the possibility of definition.

In Heidegger's theory, the failure of philosophy and theology to address the question of being results from an assumption that the word "is" has the same meaning, regardless of whether the subject is God, a human being, or the world. Heidegger's project is to examine being without regard to the characteristics of any particular being. In challenging the idea that God is the total explanation of everything that is, he seeks to understand how the possibility of existing arises, and what it actually means to "be." Heidegger points out that things come into being, exist for a while, and then pass away, and his theory gives priority to emerging and disappearing over the idea of that which is seemingly static. In focusing on the latter, Heidegger claims, philosophy has overlooked being, which in his view should be thought of as the process of coming into presence.

The philosophical analysis of being, as Heidegger interprets it, has historically been concerned with the ultimate ground of everything that is. This inquiry falls into two parts: the kind of being all things have in common; that which grounds the being of beings—the divine as the supreme being who guarantees the reality of all things. The being of beings consists in their having been created by God, who is regarded as the self-sufficient ground of all beings. Heidegger's problem with this position is that such a being is reduced to a concept in our minds—that of a particular being who can be compared with other beings. The result is that the fundamental process of coming into presence is replaced with a fixed concept of "the most universal or the highest of present beings."[2]

In his first major work, *Being and Time*, Heidegger discusses the question of being by analyzing the being of the human as it relates to the background of our everyday existence. We find ourselves having been "thrown" into the world, and facing the possibility that our death could occur at any moment.[3] Heidegger refers to the question raised by Leibniz, "Why is there anything at all rather than nothing?"[4] Whereas we normally interpret nothingness as the opposite of something, Heidegger sees a positive function for the nothing in that it enables us to realize the precariousness of our existence. We did not create ourselves and there is no necessity for us to be here. In Heidegger's words, we are "held out into the nothing."[5] We come from nothing and to nothing we will return. The being of the human is therefore described as an abyss, or a ground without a ground.

Heidegger's later work moves from an analysis of the being of humans to what he describes as being itself. He writes of a belonging together, where "being needs man ... and man belongs to being."[6] Elsewhere he defines the human as "the relationship of responding to being." Neither the individual nor being can be regarded as a separate entity or concept, but each is understood only by virtue of its relation to the other. This form of interdependence is explained as an "originary difference" underlying the distinctions between self-contained, identifiable concepts. Although depicted as an originary form of difference, it is both a sameness and a separation. Whereas in our everyday functioning we are able to recognize things as being the same or different, originary difference is a state where sameness and difference are not yet distinguished.

In his student years, Heidegger explored medieval mystical experience, particularly that of Meister Eckhart. Some of Eckhart's writing refers to God as traditionally understood, but Heidegger's interest is in the mysterious concept described by Eckhart as the Godhead. For a person to enter into the depth of this mystery, the philosophical idea of God as the highest being and the ground of all beings must be abandoned. A process of "letting-be," involving the release of the will, is then able to occur in the soul, defined as the timeless and uncreated ground of the mind. When it is still and silent, the soul becomes open to union with the ultimate mystery.[7] In such an experience, the distinction between the Godhead and creatures is overcome; there is no longer the divine and the created, but only the abyss of the nameless One.

Eckhart's concept of union with the Godhead is later compared by Heidegger with the possibility of union with being itself. In order to experience the Godhead, Eckhart seeks to transcend the theological view of God as a being. This desire, however, does not involve a rejection of traditional teaching. Eckhart writes that the Godhead "melts outwards" into the Trinity,[8] interpreted in Christian thought as God the Father, Son, and Holy Spirit. According to Heidegger, doctrines about the nature of God can be accepted in faith, but they are secondary to the question of being. Although differing from Eckhart on the question of the deity, Heidegger advocates the kind of preparation discussed by Eckhart. For Heidegger the process is one of releasing the false ideas of philosophy, renouncing the exercise of the will, and through meditative stillness, becoming open to the experience of oneness with being.

Because of the similarities involved in preparing for union with the Godhead, and the union with being that Heidegger describes, it could be assumed that what he is advocating could result in a mystical experience. Heidegger, however, rejects the categorization of his work as mysticism. One of the reasons is that although there is a mystical feeling to his work, he maintains his earlier approach by locating "being" in the world of our everyday experience. Using examples such as a jug, a bridge, and a commemorative event, Heidegger writes of the need for humans to engage in meditative thinking. His argument is that when we fail to do so, we overlook being and the hidden meaning of the things with which we are involved. A further contrast between the experience of being and that of mysticism is that for Heidegger, being is expressed within time, whereas for mystics, the unnameable God transcends the finite.

In some of his writing Heidegger acknowledges that at

particular times in history, people have had what they believed to be an experience of God, but his view that God cannot be a being results in his claim that the divine is a concept that can never be grasped. His thought lacks any commitment to faith in the God of Christianity—a belief he regards as being unduly influenced by a philosophy that seeks certainty at the expense of mystery, and the factual at the expense of the experiential. Because of the unknowable nature of the divine, and the fact that the concept of God is no longer meaningful, Heidegger discounts the possibility that people of today could have a genuine experience of the God portrayed in the sacred texts. His theory of originary difference as an ongoing mystery underlying our existence offers an alternative explanation to the idea that at a certain point, an all-powerful being created the universe out of nothing.[9]

Immanence and potentiality

Another philosopher of the twentieth century who addresses the question of being is Gilles Deleuze. His particular concern is to develop a view that is appropriate for scientific inquiry, and he draws examples from science in his writing. The position adopted by Deleuze is that the being of what we know from our experience of the world is adequate to explain ultimate reality, and that we have no need to speculate on the existence of an external, unknowable deity.

As discussed earlier in relation to Husserl, some thinkers depart from the traditional view that God is transcendent, or totally beyond us. They claim instead that God is immanent; he is within us and within his creation, though not simply identifiable with either. Deleuze rejects the idea of a transcendent God, or even of a God who is inseparable from the world. He introduces a concept of immanence that can be understood "only when immanence is no longer immanence to anything other than itself."[10] In other words, immanence absorbs everything that is;

no cause is required for anything to exist.

Deleuze links the concept of immanence to a position taken in medieval times on the question of whether the being of God is the same as the being of humans. A philosopher of that period, Duns Scotus, claimed that if we say, for example, "God is good," the quality in question would have the same meaning as it would if we were to say that a particular person is good, though there would be a difference in their respective degrees of goodness. Meister Eckhart took a contrasting view in suggesting that God's goodness is of a different kind from that of humans. The alternative proposed by Aquinas is that when we refer to the goodness of God, we are merely using an analogy based on our understanding of human goodness. In the thought of Deleuze, the qualities of being are always the same, though differences exist within a given quality. He uses an example from Scotus, who writes that a white wall containing no shapes or distinguishing marks nevertheless exhibits differing degrees or intensities of whiteness that can be demarcated from each other without affecting the quality they have in common.[11] Immanence is explained here as involving varying degrees of the same substance.

In Deleuze's theory, immanence as sameness is paradoxically a continuous differentiating process, and he outlines a concept of genesis that is interwoven with actual existence. Whereas philosophers following Kant inquire into the conditions under which our knowledge of things is possible, Deleuze describes what he regards as a prior dimension from which all reality emerges. His name for this dimension is "the virtual," and its actualization is a creative process of divergence or differentiation.[12] This fundamental activity allows each actual entity to manifest itself as something that has never before existed in exactly the way it appears at a given time. Deleuze writes, "In going from A [actual] to B [virtual] and then B to A, we do not arrive back at the point of departure as in a bare repetition."[13] Rather, the repetitive movement is described as a "progressive tour." The kind of repetition that goes back to an original starting point can only occur in the material, three-dimensional world. Although the actual would seem to be a consequence of the virtual, and therefore occurring later in time, Deleuze explains that the virtual and its actualization occur simultaneously.[14] All things have tendencies towards both the virtual and the actual, but nothing can ever reach the limit of either virtuality or actuality. An object or a being is always a "process of actualization,"[15] so that there can be no such thing as a purely actual object.

Deleuze relates the virtual to the scientific concept of chaos, which he interprets not as a simple lack of order but as a pool of resources from which new ways of thinking can emerge.[16] The virtual comprises "multiplicities," which are concrete sets of attractors or tendencies in physical processes that are continually in transition. When a system is disrupted to the extent that it is unable to maintain its original stable state, it undergoes bifurcations that abruptly change one set of attractors into another. Deleuze views the attractors as patterns for generating determinate forms in highly diverse contexts, so that the resulting actual forms need not resemble one another. The existence of endlessly bifurcating paths means that there is no limit to the set of potential divergent forms that may emerge.[17] Because of its capacity for spontaneous self-organization, the universe for Deleuze is conceived of as a creative process of becoming.

Since everything that exists is being, Deleuze does not have to ask the traditional question of how the knowing subject can reach the external object. Differences between beings or things do not involve any difference of being. The theory of difference arising from a basic repetitive process is contrasted by Deleuze with our everyday understanding of difference in relation to identity. If we say, for example, that "X is different from Y," we are assuming that X and Y are self-contained, identifiable entities. For Deleuze on the other hand, the identity of an individual thing is the consequence of a fundamental underlying difference, where through repetition, different forms of the virtual are generated. This "originary difference" is the ground of diversity and the ordinary sense of difference: "Diversity is given, but [originary] difference is that by which the given is given, that by which the given is given as diverse."[18] (This theory of originary difference has a certain similarity to that of Heidegger.) Kant had earlier claimed that the notions of space and time are not external realities, but are forms we impose on our experience of the world. Similarly for Deleuze, the virtual is neither spatial nor temporal in the conventional sense, but is the primordial event that gives rise to chronological time and three-dimensional space, and thereby to actualized, material entities.

Deleuze has no need of a God to explain the emergence of the new. In place of the idea that everything was brought into being from nothing by an eternal deity, Deleuze posits an impersonal field of pure potentiality. The existence of this field can be established through observing the effects it has in the visible world. Deleuze works backwards from what already exists to the conditions under which reality as a whole is possible.

Both Deleuze and Heidegger describe a self-sustaining creative process that is not dependent on the work of a divine being. Although Deleuze is regarded as a non-believer in the traditional sense, his writing has a quasi-mystical dimension in the oneness he describes between the virtual and the actual. Heidegger by contrast makes reference to the holy, but there is no direct connection between this idea and the central concept of his work—being.

A mystery beyond time

The Ancient Greek thinker Plato is regarded as the father of Western philosophy. Nearly all his writing is in the form of dialogue, where alternative points of view are presented. Certain themes reappear in his work, and it is reasonable to conclude that Plato favored some approaches to these issues over others. When the dialogues are taken as a whole, it would seem that Plato had a belief in some form of God, and that this concept was progressively developed throughout his work.

The society of Plato's day had begun to lose faith in the traditional gods—a situation that could have given rise to atheism. Plato's alternative approach was to develop the idea advanced by some of his predecessors that there is a connection between God or the gods and the workings of nature. In *Republic,* one of the leading characters, Socrates, claims that Homer, the greatest of the Ancient Greek epic poets, tells lies about the gods.[19] In order to account for the varied and contradictory experiences of life and the natural world, Homer had presented many different gods, each with specific powers and spheres of influence. He also portrayed them as having disagreements among themselves and being morally defective. Socrates counters that God is one, and the absolute source of truth and goodness.

In the thought of Plato there are two worlds: the one we see, consisting of separate material things that change and die, and one we cannot see, which is eternal and indivisible. It contains the forms or paradigms, defined as the pure essences of the things around us. The forms have an important role in *Timaeus,* which is a dialogue giving a mythical account of the creation of the universe. At that period of Greek history, what we now call "myths" bore no relation to the idea of things that are merely made up. Myths were seen rather as stories that unveiled truth and were of particular value in situations where human thought processes fail. The Creator in *Timaeus* is portrayed as a divine Craftsman who looks to the eternal paradigm, and makes the universe as a copy of the perfect original.[20]

The creative process described in the dialogue involves two

kinds of causes. In addition to the work of the Craftsman, there is already in existence visible matter consisting of the four basic elements, earth, air, fire and water, which is said to be moving in an irregular and disorderly manner. The properties of the elements are determined by their constitutions, and cannot be changed. Nevertheless, the Craftsman is able to take the materials he has received, and to bring order out of disorder. He also desires that the world should be a god, having an intelligence of its own, and he therefore creates the soul. This is formed from both the eternal realm of indivisible being, and the transient, divisible being that is associated with physical bodies. The universe is then formed within the soul, the two being joined at their respective centers. This "world soul" is diffused throughout the body of the universe, and is seen as a living being, containing both the sameness of the indivisible and the difference of the divisible.[21] Furthermore, since the universe itself was believed to be eternal, and the world soul is given the status of a god, it, too, is seen as eternal. Time and the heavenly bodies are then included within the acts of creation. The Craftsman and the world soul can be regarded as two aspects of the one God, the former representing changelessness, order and design, and the latter representing movement and life. A difficulty arises, however, in reconciling the idea of a Craftsman who creates the world soul, with that of the world soul having always existed. This situation is addressed in the dialogue by the presentation of a second account of creation.

Plato begins this new account by referring to the elements that were brought into an orderly state by the Craftsman. Prior to this act, the elements had consisted merely of faint traces. Rather than being already distinguished as individual things, as had been assumed in the first account, these traces move in cycles of transformation, one merging into the other. Because they have not yet become elements, a place has to be found for the traces that is beyond the forms and beyond the physical world. The Greek word for place is *chora,* and Plato uses this term in outlining a mysterious state that is prior to creation and to the advent of time and space. It thereby provides a context for the earlier ideas of the world soul being created on the one hand, and of its having always existed on the other.

Although *chora* is indestructible, it is said to be "hardly real."[22] It is neither being itself nor a particular being, but is that which enables being to occur. Plato describes it as the "nurse of all becoming." *Chora* has no form and is invisible, yet it "appears" by taking the form of the traces it receives. Its function is to provide a fleeting home for this proto-material, yet it cannot be in any location since it has no being of its own. It is moved and shaped by the entering traces, so that it appears differently at different times. In parts of the dialogue Plato likens *chora* to an empty space, but at other places the concept is depicted as being like unformed matter. Because it is indeterminate and formless, *chora* is able to give birth to what will become the elements and ultimately the cosmos itself.

In a later dialogue, *Sophist,* Plato's thought undergoes a modification in that the forms are no longer seen as isolated and self-enclosed, but as having the power to act or be acted upon. A form is now understood as being in relation, as well as being in itself. Whether formal or material, beings can only exist if they are in relation to other things. On that basis, living beings are described as "nothing but power."[23] It is also proposed in Plato's later work that there must be a cause that keeps the universe in motion, physical matter being unable to move itself, and that anything capable of self-motion must be alive.[24] Since the world soul alone has the power of self-movement, it is depicted as the principle of life.

The concept of living things as power is taken up by the process philosopher Alfred North Whitehead who suggests that the being of any living entity is its potential for becoming. Process thought disputes the traditional view that God is all-powerful, all-knowing, absolutely perfect and therefore unchangeable.[25] These doctrines are replaced with the idea that God and the world are inter-related; God is in the world and the world is in God. (This theory is "panentheism," as distinct from pantheism, which holds that God and the world are identical.) Both God and finite beings draw on the same eternal source of power and creativity. From this it follows that God is dynamic, and changes through experiencing the universe in its own creative development. The nature of his involvement with humans leads Whitehead to describe God as "the great companion—the fellow-sufferer who understands."[26] As is the case with Plato, Whitehead sees two aspects in God: one is formal and unchanging, and includes his characteristics such as goodness and wisdom; the other is continually in process as God is affected by everything that happens in the universe.

The portrayal of creation in *Timaeus* addresses the problem that has been discussed in much of Western philosophy, which is to explain how thought is connected to matter, or in Plato's words, how the realm of eternal, indivisible being can relate to the transient, divisible, physical world. His initial approach is to posit the existence of a divine Craftsman who is restricted to working with existing material. Plato then moves to discussing an underlying mystery, *chora,* which is prior to the world as we know it. *Chora* contains no divisions, since everything within it is merely potential. Its activity is the underlying condition for the formation of matter and thus of individual things, giving rise in turn to a world that is comprehended on the basis of distinctions.

Both Plato and Whitehead reject the idea that an all-powerful God created the universe out of nothing. But whereas Whitehead sees the eternal creative process itself as primordial, Plato did not attempt to reconcile the idea of a living, eternal Creator with his concept of *chora.* The reason would seem to be that in his view the deity is, at least in principle, comprehensible, whereas *chora* is beyond our powers of thinking as creatures in a three-dimensional world. With regard to the overall question of God, the choice is between a belief in reality itself as an eternal creative process, or in a God who has always existed, and who, at a certain point, decides to bring everything into being. If, as Whitehead suggests, God and finite beings draw on the same source of creativity, that source would seem to be adequate as an explanation of the totality of existence, and would not need to be supplemented by the idea of a divine being who makes some kind of connection with the creative process itself.

Summary

The thought of Heidegger and Deleuze contains the idea that the coming into being of the universe is not the result of a singular action by an all-powerful being, but is an ongoing, self-sustaining process that is beyond our powers of comprehension. Plato in *Timaeus* adopts a similar position with respect to his concept of *chora*. Each of the accounts suggests an indeterminate realm of potential from which arises our existence as beings in time and space.

In the next chapter we will look at the difficulties that arise as a result of the conflicting philosophical views on the arguments both for God's existence, and whether or not a personal relationship can be established with the divine.

1 Heidegger, "Letter on Humanism," *Martin Heidegger: Basic Writings*, ed. David F. Krell (New York: Harper & Row, 1977), 218.

2 ________, *Early Greek Thinking*, tr. David F. Krell and F.A. Capuzzi, (New York: Harper & Row, 1975), 50.

3 ________, *Being and Time*, tr. John Macquarrie and Edward Robinson, (Oxford: Blackwell, 1962), 174.

4 ________, *An Introduction to Metaphysics,* tr. Ralph Manhein, (New Haven: Yale University Press, 1973), 1.

5 ________, "What is Metaphysics?", *Martin Heidegger: Pathmarks*, ed. William McNeill, (Cambridge: Cambridge University Press, 1998), 91.

6 _______, *Contributions to Philosophy (From Enowning)*, trans. Parvis Emad and Kenneth Maly (Bloomington: Indiana University Press, 1999), 177.

7 James M. Clark and John V. Skinner, (ed. and trans.), *Meister Eckhart: Selected Treatises and Sermons*, (London: Faber & Faber, 1958), Q, 238.

8 Reza Shah-Kazemi, *Paths to Transcendence: According to Shankara, Ibn Arabi, and Meister Eckhart* (Bloomington: World Wisdom Inc., 2006), 165.

9 It should be noted that there have always been believers from the various traditions who do not accept this view of creation. Instead, they hold that something was already in existence before God's creative act. (See Chapter 8 for comments on this position.)

10 Deleuze, *Pure Immanence: Essays on a Life*, tr. Anne Boyman, (New York: Zone Books, 2001), 26.

11 ______, *Expressionism in Philosophy: Spinoza*, trans. Martin Joughin (New York: Zone Books, 1990), 197.

12 ______, *Difference and Repetition*, tr. Paul Patton, (New York: Columbia University Press, 1994), 212.

13 Ibid., 208.

14 Deleuze, "The Actual and the Virtual," tr. Eliot Ross Albert, in Gilles Deleuze and Claire Parnet, *Dialogues II*, tr. Hugh Tomlinson and Barbara Habberjam (New York: Columbia University Press, 1987), 149.

15 _______, *Pure Immanence: Essays on a Life*, 31.

16 _______ and Félix Guattari, *What Is Philosophy?* (London: Verso, 1994), 118.

17 Manuel De Landa, *Intensive Science and Virtual Philosophy*, (London: Continuum, 2004), 21.

18 Deleuze, (1987), 222.

19 *The Republic of Plato,* ed. James Adam (Cambridge: Cambridge University Press, 2009), 389B.

20 *Plato's Timaeus,* tr. Francis M. Cornford, ed. Oskar Piest (Indianapolis: Bobbs-Merrill, 1959), 27C (hereafter cited as T).

21 T, 34A–35A.

22 T, 52A–D.

23 *Plato's Theory of Knowledge,* tr. Francis M. Cornford, (New York: Dover Publications, 2003), 247E.

24 *The Laws of Plato,* tr. Thomas L. Pangle (Chicago: University of Chicago Press, 1988), 895c.

25 Charles Hartshorne, *Omnipotence and other Theological Mistakes,* (Albany: State University of New York Press, 1984), 2.

26 Alfred North Whitehead, *Process and Reality* (New York: Macmillan, 1929), p. 532.

Chapter 7

An Uncertain Question

Throughout much of recorded history, philosophers have sought to evaluate the evidence for and against the idea that a personal God not only exists, but possesses the kinds of qualities that enable a relationship with him to be established. The adoption of a particular faith generally involves an acceptance of the truth of the sacred texts on which that faith is based. These concern the moral failings of human beings, and the remedy offered in terms of God's forgiveness, love and care.

Alongside the belief in a given set of teachings, arguments have been presented for the existence of a divine being that do not depend on the communications that are believed to have occurred between the deity and selected individuals, but rely instead on humans' ability to reason. These approaches, some of which emerged in the medieval period, include the idea that the whole of reality can be attributed to an ultimate cause, or to the creative activity of an all-powerful designer. More recently, it has been claimed that the limitations of our reasoning processes indicate the need for a God who gives meaning to the world and ourselves.

Certain philosophers attempt to validate religious doctrines through their reliance on reason. Descartes proposes that because he cannot doubt his own existence, he is similarly free from doubt regarding the idea of a supremely perfect being. For Locke, the concepts of Heaven and Hell are justified on the grounds that they are necessary to promote moral behavior, and he argues that the resurrection of Jesus from the dead ensures the possibility of eternal life. In the thought of Leibniz, the goodness of God's creation reflects the idea that something actual has a greater degree of perfection than something merely possible. The resurrection of Jesus is then interpreted as a divine act that enabled a human body to achieve a more perfect form.

On the question of God's existence, equal weight has at times been given to conclusions based on the exercise of reason, and those arising from the experience of faith. But even among thinkers who place a high value on the former, a basic orientation towards the spiritual may lead them to give greater credence to the insights arising from their religious experience than to their rational conclusions. Descartes claimed to have received his ideas in a vision, and he describes divine revelation of this kind as being more certain than knowledge acquired through his reasoning abilities. Husserl regards the immediate awareness of God as prior to any evidence that could be advanced for his existence. Faith that comes from the heart and will has a more profound significance for this philosopher than ideas originating in the mind.

Regarding the nature of God and his relationship with us, a variety of views can be seen in the writings of the theistic philosophers. Kant, for example, regards God as a morally commanding being who can be addressed in prayer, but who cannot be the subject of human love. Pascal accepts the doctrine that God has selected certain individuals for salvation, and on that basis, he would see himself as a recipient of divine favor. For Kierkegaard, God is an unknown who does not provide us with any evidence for his existence; the only thing we can do is to risk everything by committing ourselves to the paradox of the God-man, and trusting that we may eventually discover it to be true. A contrasting position is taken by Marion, who holds that we cannot reach out to God, but that he takes the initiative in acts of self-revelation that are experienced as overwhelming.

An individual's religious experience will inevitably be affected by the kind of characteristics the deity is believed to possess, and the conditions under which access to him is said to be possible. This situation contrasts with the kind of relationships we form with other human beings, where we come to understand their thought processes, their values, their emotional responses and so on. Although a relationship with God is held to be an essential part of belief, the only information we have about him that would be relevant to such a relationship is contained in the sacred texts.

The various deficits in our knowledge of God are justified on the grounds that we must exercise faith. A problem here is the absence of consistent and persuasive evidence on which such faith can be based. Apart from the philosophers already discussed, many of the greatest minds in human history have reached widely differing conclusions about the nature of God and what he requires of us.

A sense of connectedness to God, in association with a rational acceptance that such a being is necessary to explain reality as a whole, would inevitably lead an individual to have no doubts regarding his existence. On the other hand, if a person were not convinced by the arguments based on reason, or by the teachings presented in the sacred texts, it would be difficult for her to trust in the reported experiences of others in the hope of becoming convinced that God does in fact exist. A different situation can arise where a person is persuaded by the evidence and commits herself in faith to God, but where she fails to experience anything of the life transformation that is said to be the long-term outcome of such a commitment. As a result, such a person may have reason to doubt that a relationship with the divine has actually been established.

In the case of someone without a religious background who is seeking the truth about God, the primary need will be to identify the true deity and what he requires of us. Even if it were the case, as claimed by some theists, that there is only one God who is known by different names, there are considerable variations in the way the demands he makes on his creatures have been understood by his followers. These concern the facts that must be accepted about him, together with the personal qualities and experiences of the individual that would indicate the existence of a genuine relationship with the divine. Added to this are the different behaviors and rituals that are prescribed for the promotion of spiritual development. When faced with the prospect of choosing a deity, an individual may examine the different biblical texts in an attempt to determine which is most likely to represent the truth, or she may observe believers from the respective traditions as to the quality of the lives they lead. The selection of a particular God may result in the person's incorporation into a certain religious and social culture, and will generally involve the belief that those who have chosen differently will not receive the favor of the one true God, or at worst will be condemned.

Certain accounts given by mystics and discussed by negative theologians involve contact with a dimension that is beyond the ability of language to describe. Some theorists interpret such phenomena as representing contact with the divine, thereby serving as a confirmation of his existence. It has been suggested in earlier chapters that the reality accessed by mystics is a feature of the universe itself rather than pointing to the existence of a personal God. The question then arises as to whether a person who regards the universe as being the ultimate reality could receive all the benefits that are claimed to occur in the lives of traditional believers. Furthermore, an explanation is required for the fact that countless people in the history of the monotheisms have experienced the kind of life transformation that is both meaningful to the individuals concerned, and finds expression in loving attitudes towards others. (These issues will be addressed in Chapter 13.)

In this section of the book, it has been suggested that the existence of God cannot be proved through reason only, or through reason in combination with revelation and personal experience based on that which has been revealed. The following section proposes a compatibility between a view of the universe that has emerged in scientific inquiry, and an interpretation of ultimate reality that is reflected in the experience of mystics. The arguments advanced cannot prove that a personal God external to the cosmos does not exist, but the parallels between mysticism and scientific discoveries suggest that no all-powerful being is required to explain the creative process. This claim is substantiated by evidence that the universe is self-sustaining and may have always existed.

Section 2

God and Science

Chapter 8

The Infinite Universe

Quantum theory

One of the most important scientific discoveries of recent times concerns the nature of matter.

It had previously been thought that any physical substance could be continually divided until the smallest unit, the atom, was reached. Because of its indivisibility, the atom was considered to be the basic building block of the universe. Investigations early in the twentieth century revealed that atoms are composed of particles; the central nucleus of the atom contains protons and neutrons and is surrounded by orbiting electrons. During the same period, experiments in the study of light, which was originally thought to consist either of particles or of electromagnetic waves, revealed that light has both wave-like and particle-like properties. Subsequently it has been shown that under given conditions, matter and light exhibit the behavior of either waves or particles.

To illustrate the above, if a wave of water were to move towards a screen containing two vertical slits, the new waves created on the far side of the screen would interfere with each other, forming the kind of pattern that occurs when ocean waves meet. In the case of electrons, and indeed of particles in general, it was originally thought that if they were fired at the same kind of screen and a detector panel were placed a further distance away, the pattern of the particles on the detector would more or less correspond to the size and shape of the slits. It was discovered, however, that when electrons are fired, even individually and with time gaps in between, they interfere with each other, forming a pattern on the detector resembling that of intersecting waves. But then if a measuring device is placed between the screen and the detector, particles that are fired will be seen to have passed through one slit or the other, so that no interference pattern is formed. When it is not observed, a given wave spreads out over an immeasurable distance, but the process of detecting it makes it appear as though it is a particle in a specific place. Observation, it is said, causes the wave to "collapse" into a particle state.

The significance of measurement in examining the nature of the wave/particle was revealed in an experiment involving particles separated by distance. Properties of a particle include spin, which can be up or down, left or right. Particles can become entangled through close proximity to each other, which means that in any subsequent observation they will be found to have opposite spins. Until a particle is measured, however, it contains all possible states simultaneously. When two entangled particles fly off in opposite directions and one of them is measured, that particle takes on a definite value, for example, a left spin. The process of measuring instantaneously determines the state of the other particle, which will be found to have a right spin. This result occurs even in situations where the particles are separated at a distance that would require a communication between them to travel faster than the speed of light. Einstein's theory of special relativity states that matter cannot reach this speed, but in the 1980s a French physicist, Alain Aspect, was able to demonstrate an immediate "communication" between particles at the moment of measurement, and he showed that this would be the case even if the particles were separated by light years. The same results were obtained in experiments conducted by Nicolas Gisin and his colleagues in Geneva in 1997.[1] Rather than being a transgression of the speed of light, these findings suggested that particles could no longer be regarded as having definite locations. This led to an interest among physicists in the possibility that the universe contains more than three spatial dimensions, and that a "higher" dimension could account for the instantaneous connection between seemingly distant particles.[2]

The wave/particle duality revealed in acts of measurement, together with the interconnectedness that exists between particles that appear to be separated by distance, resulted in a view that the entire universe is an undivided whole.[3] Because they have no actual location, the particles of which we and all other objects are made are seen as having an intrinsic connectedness, the normal separateness we observe being merely an abstraction. It had earlier been assumed that the various properties of an object, down to and including its atoms, could be determined precisely, and that any act of observation would have no effect on the results. But the concept of an indivisible universe means that no ultimate separation can exist between an observer who conducts an experiment, the apparatus used, and the findings obtained. Beyond the self-contained identities of our daily existence is a mysterious unity from which all individual phenomena arise. (These findings are discussed later in relation to the separateness that is claimed to exist between God, human beings, and the natural world.)

The Big Bang Theory

A scientific theory with implications for religious belief concerns the origins of the universe. Monotheists generally attribute this to God's act of creation—an idea that has been linked by certain religious authorities to the concept of the Big Bang.[4] Scientists describe this event as an explosion that brought everything into being from nothing.

In the 1920s, the astronomer Edwin Hubble studied the light that is received on earth from distant galaxies and discovered that it had longer wavelengths than that studied in a laboratory. The light from the galaxies was found to be at the red end of the electromagnetic color spectrum that goes from red to violet.[5] When there is an increase in the distance between a measured object and the point of observation, the expansion in wavelength that results from the movement is described as "redshift." By contrast, a "blueshift" occurs in the case of an approaching body, which has a shorter wavelength. (This principle applies in a similar manner to sound waves, where a horn blown from an approaching train has a higher pitch than the one heard when the train is receding.) Waves are compressed by a forward motion and expanded by a receding motion. Whether a star is approaching or receding can be determined by measuring the extent of its blueshift or redshift. On the basis of the redshift he observed, Hubble concluded that the galaxies at the greatest distance from earth are moving away from each other and from the earth at a faster rate than the ones closer to us.

An expanding universe implies that at some time in the past, all the matter and energy forming the universe must have originated in a single point. According to the standard Big Bang theory, this point of contraction was characterized by near infinite heat temperature and material density. Since the laws of mathematics and physics cannot be applied to such a unique event, science itself is unable to explain its origin. It is claimed that the cause was a "random quantum fluctuation"[6] that resulted in a gigantic explosion in which all the particles forming the early universe flew outwards in all directions. This approach seemed to be confirmed in 1963, when the astronomers Arno Penzias and Robert Wilson discovered the existence of a background radiation that was claimed to be the consequence of a vast explosion.

In the standard interpretation of the Big Bang theory, the initial explosion was followed by an enormous expansion in which the universe doubled in size many times over within a fraction of a second. Matter and energy were evenly distributed, so that the universe is generally described as "smooth." Furthermore, since it is believed to be governed by Euclidean geometry, the universe is described as "flat."[7] (In this form of mathematics, parallel lines never intersect, in contrast to the geometry of curved matter or curved space, where lines draw closer and then intersect.[8]) The expansion of the universe within the first second of the Big Bang was caused by inflationary energy, which was then transformed into hot plasma—a form of gas. As the plasma cooled, the rate of expansion slowed. One million years after the Big Bang, the temperature was low enough for nuclei and electrons to coalesce in the formation of atoms. Then after a billion years, under the influence of gravity, matter clumped together to form galaxies, stars and planets. A rapid increase in the expansion rate occurred at about nine billion years after the Big Bang. The cause was attributed to an anti-gravity force that was given the name "dark energy."

A further concept that has been incorporated within the Big Bang theory is "dark matter." Stars and galaxies are held together by gravity, so that the larger the mass, the greater the gravity strength. It was discovered that there is not enough matter in the universe to account for the amount of gravity that would be needed to hold the galaxies in place. The conclusion was reached that hidden from our view are vast quantities of nonluminous or dark matter that exert the amount of gravity required to maintain the orderly movements of the cosmos.

It is believed that since the time of the Big Bang, the universe has been continuously expanding, and that it will probably do so indefinitely. An alternative view is that the expansion phase will eventually cease and be replaced by one of contraction, leading ultimately to a "big crunch." In either of these events, at some point life will come to an end.

Alternative approaches

In casting doubt on the validity of the Big Bang theory, some scientists have suggested that the universe is a self-creative process. They accept the recent idea put forward by mathematical cosmologists that the universe is multidimensional, which means it extends beyond the three dimensions with which we are familiar.[9] Because we are conditioned by the limits of this form of existence, it is difficult for us to comprehend the nature of this higher dimensional reality. The dimensions we know are of course length, width and height (or thickness). But if it were possible for us to conceive of a two-dimensional form of existence that involved only width and length, a being who lived in this "square" land would be unable to imagine what it would be like to exist in our three-dimensional "cube" world, where movements up and down are possible, in addition to movements sideways, forwards and backwards. We find ourselves in a similar situation when we try to envisage higher dimensions that would incorporate the three we know, while at the same time extending beyond them.

One of the earliest investigations of higher dimensions came in the 1970s, when it was proposed that the basic building blocks of the universe are strings that vibrate at different frequencies and interact with each other in a variety of ways. Through these processes they give rise to different forms of matter and energy. Originally it was thought that strings had only one dimension—length. But because of the mathematical problems associated with a single dimension, the conclusion was reached that in addition to strings, sheets called membranes or "branes," which are strings of two or more dimensions, must also exist.[10] It was then found that when this theory was applied to a three-dimensional universe, it could not account for the existence of gravity but only for the other three fundamental forces of nature: electromagnetism, the strong nuclear force that binds protons and neutrons in forming the nucleus of atoms, and the weak nuclear force that is responsible for the radioactive decay of subatomic particles. Gravity had been explained in one of Einstein's theories, where it was applied to the earth, the solar system and the universe as a whole. What was missing in the string theory picture was a theory of quantum gravity that would determine the nature of physical reality at the smallest possible scale. It was only when string theory was applied to a ten-dimensional universe that gravity could be included. The result was a mathematical unification of the four forces of nature in what is known as the "unified field theory." In the mid-1990s, string theorists reached agreement that there are ten dimensions of space and one of time.

The following is a brief summary of four contemporary approaches that describe the universe as a continuing creative process based on its multidimensional structure.[11] The authors' areas of concern with regard to the standard theory include its reliance on a chance event, the inadequate period of time allowed for the universe to become smooth and flat, an assumption that there is no subquantum domain to explain the existence of quantum phenomena, an uncertainty as to whether the universe will expand forever or end in a big crunch, a problematic account of black holes, a failure to address string theory, and an inadequate understanding of the quantum vacuum.

(1) Paul Steinhardt and Neil Turok

In their work *Endless Universe,*[11] the authors propose that the universe is cyclical, and that it does not require the kind of beginning point contained in the standard Big Bang theory. Steinhardt and Turok develop an idea from string theory that the visible universe lies on a brane consisting of four dimensions of space-time. On the other side of a fifth dimension is a brane containing a parallel universe that is a mirror image of our own, but is beyond our field of vision. The two branes are able to move across the fifth dimension, either towards each other or away from each other. This dimension contains dark energy in a potential form. Through an infinite cyclic process, a collision of the branes occurs at regular intervals. The background radiation that has been attributed to the Big Bang would then be seen as a residue from an earlier collision in a previously existing universe.

As is the case with the standard theory, in the model presented by the authors, there is a period where dark energy predominates and the universe expands at an accelerating rate, causing cosmic matter to thin out. But whereas in the standard view, the expansion is generally thought to continue forever, Steinhardt and Turok suggest that after about a trillion years, the dark energy begins to decay, causing the expansion to decrease and eventually come to a halt. At this point the dark energy becomes a high-pressure gas and spreads out evenly across space. Because the anti-gravity effect is reversed, the fifth dimension begins to contract and the two branes move slowly towards each other. In addition to this interbrane force, gravity from the other brane provides energy for the contraction. When the two branes eventually collide, they are still stretched out, which means that the extremely hot and dense matter resulting from the collision cannot be infinite, as is the case with the Big Bang theory. The explosion of matter and radiation leads to the formation of galaxies, as in the standard model. Then follows a lengthy period of acceleration caused by dark energy. This comes to an end upon the decaying of the energy, as explained above. The cyclic process outlined will continue indefinitely. Since the universe is estimated to be about 13.7 billion years old, from the perspective of the Steinhardt-Turok theory, we have reached that point of time in the present cycle.

According to the authors, one of the strengths of their model is that unlike the standard theory, it does not require the inclusion of inflationary energy, which is a chance event that is said to have included properties exactly tuned to spread matter and radiation evenly throughout the universe. Furthermore, the inflationary energy described must have decayed in exactly the right way to create the variations within the plasma that enabled the formation of galaxies. The initial point of contraction in the standard theory must itself have been a random event that consisted of both the potential for the short-lived inflation, and the seeds of the dark energy that would not manifest until nine billion years later. Whereas the authors' model requires only one form of acceleration in one period per cycle, the standard theory has two forms: one that cannot be explained, and the other that was not anticipated by the theory itself. The rate of acceleration being proposed is vastly lower than that assumed in the first period of inflation—a fraction of a second, and it is claimed by the authors that the universe could not have become smooth and flat within such a minute period of time. Furthermore, in the authors' theory, the features of smoothness and flatness are due to the effect of dark energy that predominated for a trillion years or so.

Steinhardt and Turok argue that the ideas of the Big Bang, a rapid inflationary period, and dark energy, when taken together lack coherence, and for that reason they provide an unlikely explanation of the origins of the universe. Furthermore, since the standard model cannot explain the past, it cannot be relied upon to predict the future. Opinions differ as to whether dark energy will last forever, or whether it will eventually cease, leading ultimately to a crunch. According to the authors, the theory they propose has the advantage of requiring no such beginning or ending to the story, since the universe is involved in a cyclical process that is infinite and self-sustaining.

(2) Paul LaViolette

In *Subquantum Kinetics: A Systems Approach,* the author suggests that beneath the level of particles is a subquantum realm that continually creates matter and energy.[13] LaViolette's ideas are based on general system theory, which states that a system as a whole is greater than the sum of the parts of which it is comprised, and that the parts and the system mutually affect each other, thereby acquiring new properties in a continuing evolutionary process.

It is generally accepted that the universe obeys the laws of thermodynamics. The first of these prescribes that in a closed system, energy can be changed from one form into another, but cannot be created or destroyed; the total amount of matter and energy remains constant. A further characteristic of closed systems is contained in the second law, which states that such systems become increasingly disordered. In this context, "order" indicates a pattern of separate, well-defined areas. When a system is disordered, the areas merge with each other so that their differences disappear. For example, a cold object placed in a hot container will eventually achieve a thermal equilibrium with its environment. Whereas the conventional view is that the universe is a closed system, the theory outlined below describes an open system that produces order. Matter and energy are continually created, the known physical universe being part of a larger invisible system.

It was originally believed that light waves are carried through the medium of an ether. These waves, it was claimed, do not arise from the ether itself but are moved by oscillating mechanical stresses communicated through the medium. The concept of an ether was later replaced by quantum field theory. This deals with systems containing many particles and enables both particles and fields to be analyzed within the one theoretical framework. Quantum theory taken as a whole retains the idea of a mechanical function—hence it is often referred to as quantum mechanics.

A limitation of the conventional approach is that acts of measurement involve the use of probes consisting of matter or energy. This means it is only other matter or energy that can be accessed. There is no direct way of ascertaining the possibility of a subquantum domain that could explain the existence of subatomic particles and energy waves. In contrast to the accepted view of the universe as a closed system, the theory presented by the author is that as an open system, the physical or explicit order is explained by an unobservable implicit order consisting of processes beyond the physical. Rather than being a vacuum, this subquantum world is an ether consisting of etheric particles or etherons. Unlike the earlier view of the ether as merely a carrier of mechanical force, the subquantum ether changes through interacting with its particles. These are of different types, each forming a particular substrate. The etherons that are given the name X and Y are interrelated and give rise to positive and negative electric potential at the subatomic level; G etherons have a similar formative role with regard to gravity potential.

The whole of reality has generally been held to consist of various forms of quantum phenomena. In the subquantum view, space in its entirety is formed by the ether. Conventional quantum theory considers subatomic particles to be closed systems, whereas for LaViolette, the particle consists of a wave pattern that is continually affected by the influx of etherons. Furthermore, the particle has been regarded either as a point or as a moving wave, depending on the experimental conditions. In subquantum theory by contrast, a particle consists of varying concentrations of the X, Y, and G substrates. It has both wave and particle features since the X and Y etherons can form either as material particles or as photons, which are waves of electromagnetic energy that can take the form of particles of light. Subatomic particles arising spontaneously from the activity of the etherons serve as sites for the creation of further particles throughout space. This process occurs most rapidly within stars and massive objects at the core of galaxies. New cosmic bodies are formed when a "mother" star expels matter and radiates energy.

Another aspect of the standard theory concerns the existence of black holes that are found throughout the universe. They are believed to be the result of stars collapsing when they run out of fuel. The energy and matter swirling around a black hole is described as an accretion disc. It has a speed and density that causes the emission of radiation in the shape of spirals. The cores of spiral galaxies are thought to be black holes, but the idea that matter could be created and expelled from them is countered by the conventional view that this material is continually being recycled back into the black hole and is thus consumed by its gravity. Against this claim, LaViolette argues that only outward movement has ever been observed from accretion discs. Furthermore, if the surrounding material were drawn inward, the nature of the momentum it acquired would force it to orbit at a distance, thereby overriding any gravitational pull.

Astronomical measurements taken early in the twentieth century indicated that most of the galaxies exhibit redshift, which resulted in the commonly accepted view that the universe began with an explosion and has been expanding ever since. Shortly after these discoveries, a theory was advanced that the observed redshift is a consequence of photons losing energy while traveling through the intergalactic gravitational field, rather than being an effect of an expanding universe. LaViolette endorses this latter view, proposing that both the ether and the galaxies are non-expanding and cosmically stationary. Since matter and energy are continually being created, there is no need for a massive explosion to explain the existence of redshift.

The accepted explanation for the fast yet regular movement of stars and galaxies is based on the assumption that there is not enough matter in the visible universe to provide the amount of gravity needed for everything to be held in place. Accordingly, the existence of invisible or dark matter has been proposed in order to account for the stability of cosmic bodies, galaxies, and clusters of galaxies. In the 1990s, several clusters were analyzed for their gravitational mass—a figure that is calculated on the basis of gravitational attraction for other bodies. It was found that the visible mass of the clusters was sufficient to explain the measured velocities, so that the existence of dark matter is not required. Also, in recent years astronomers have found that the areas between the galaxies contain far more matter than had previously been thought. This means that the universe has a greater density than that described in the standard theory. The alternative outlined by LaViolette is that this density is the result of a continual creative process.

Although coexisting with the subatomic particles in three spatial dimensions, the etherons also constitute a fourth dimension of space-time. A fifth dimension enfolds the other four. In the author's view, the universe is continually being recreated through the activity of the etherons. No single event is required to explain the origin of matter; it has existed for countless billions of years.

(3) Manjir Samanta-Laughton

According to this author, black holes are the ultimate source of creation.[14] Her ideas conflict with the generally accepted view that the center of a black hole is an area of infinite density and infinite gravity that causes surrounding material to be sucked in and lost forever. It is believed that nothing can escape from black holes, not even light. Their existence is inferred from the observation of quasars, which are massive distant objects surrounded by matter and energy that swirl around them in spirals. Jets of electrons moving at just below the speed of light are emitted at an angle perpendicular to the black hole and the quasar.

As discussed above, string theory outlines the existence of ten spatial dimensions. The three with which we are familiar are based on the speed of light (c), and the idea being proposed by the author is that the dimension above our own exists at the frequency of the speed of light squared (c^2).[15] Light comes from higher dimensions and passes through the c^2 realm, slowing down when it enters the c region. At the point of a black hole, the light splits into matter, which then becomes our three-dimensional universe, and antimatter, which constitutes the

c^2 dimension beyond space and time. This movement of light would explain the direction and speed of the electron jets emitted from quasars. The total matter and energy of the universe originate in the passage of light from an infinite source, and the unseen parts of the universe, conventionally described as dark matter and dark energy, exist in this higher dimensional light. Similarly black holes, rather than being dark and all-devouring, enable light to enter our dimension, and are thus the source of the endless creative process.

(4) David Bohm and Basil Hiley

The earliest formulation of quantum theory was that of the Danish physicist Niels Bohr (1885–1962), and his interpretation has become the standard for most scientists today. In discussing the wave/particle paradox revealed in the two-slit experiment, Bohr draws a sharp distinction between the microscopic world of quantum phenomena, and the macroscopic or classical world of our everyday experience. Since the former does not possess any definite properties until a measurement is made, Bohr suggests that we cannot say anything about the nature and behavior of particles. The overall experimental situation in his view should be seen as an indivisible and unanalyzable whole. In quantum physics generally, the state of a particle is defined as its "wave function," which is the mathematical probability that the particle when measured will be found in a given location. Although the wave function has the same mathematical structure as that of a physical wave, in Bohr's theory, the knowledge of quantum reality is limited to a statistical probability.[16]

The approach of Bohm and Hiley seeks to understand the actual functioning of particles and waves. They argue that a limitation on human knowledge does not imply a limitation on the reality of the microscopic world, and that the concept of a real quantum wave should be maintained. What they propose is significant when considering the Big Bang theory, where the initial explosion is believed to have caused a massive spread of particles. Yet in that situation, matter would have been able to form without the presence of an observer or a measuring device. Furthermore, three-dimensional beings or objects, for example, the scientist and the equipment, are composed ultimately of quantum phenomena. On those grounds the authors challenge the idea that the experimental setup can be divided into the reality of the classical world and the unreality of the quantum.

Following the position adopted by Bohr, scientists have tended to ignore the vast amounts of energy that exist in the quantum vacuum. Such energy, it is claimed, cannot be measured by instruments and therefore should not be regarded as real. The authors' view is that the vacuum is the ground for everything that exists. With regard to the two-slit experiment, they suggest that the electron is an actual particle accompanied by a new kind of quantum wave or field that spreads out over the whole of space. Unlike the electromagnetic field, this new field is not associated with a force. Rather, it consists of information that is potentially active in all areas, becoming actual only in the particle's immediate environment. Bohr holds that a particle somehow passes through both slits and creates an interference pattern. In Bohm and Hiley's theory, only the quantum wave follows this route, while the particle is guided by the wave as to which slit it will pass through.

Scientists have generally regarded the physical world as the fundamental reality. The view proposed by the authors is that beyond what we know lies an unseen dimension—the "implicate order."[16] In one sense this concept coincides with the conventional understanding of the quantum vacuum, but the authors have expanded the description in their theory that the implicate order continuously enfolds everything, and unfolds into the "explicate order," which is the manifest world of our everyday existence. The non-local connections that were revealed in experiments involving the spin of correlated but distant particles indicate that unlike the material world, the implicate order is indivisible. Things in the explicate order appear to be separate and continuous in that they have observable starting and finishing points. Quantum phenomena on the other hand were found to be discontinuous when it was discovered that the electron can only occupy certain orbits around the atom's nucleus and cannot move gradually between one orbit and another.

For Bohm and Hiley, the universe is an inseparable, multidimensional whole. The implicate order contains all the possibilities and potentialities of the visible world, and it determines which of these will become actual at any given time. Each unfolded element expresses in a unique way the totality of the whole. It may have happened that billions of years ago, a particular process of unfolding occurred, where an explosion followed by a massive expansion resulted in the universe as we know it. The authors argue that from our perspective today, such an event might seem like a Big Bang, but in the larger context, it could be just one of many ripples from the implicate order that occur over lengthy periods of time—perhaps extending to infinity.[17]

Language and the unknown

The various theorists who discuss the dimensions beyond those of our immediate awareness are limited to the language of our three-dimensional existence. Since these dimensions transcend space and time, words such as "up," "down," "high" and "low" cannot be understood as indicating a particular direction. LaViolette refers to an implicit dimension that gives rise to the visible world, and he uses the term "subquantum" to describe it. The use of the prefix "sub" could suggest that what he is referring to is in some sense below the world we know. His theory shows, however, that because of the complexity of the dimensions involved, any directional term would have no real meaning.

In addition to their reservations about the Big Bang theory, the above writers claim that the existence of higher dimensions is essential to our understanding of the physical world. The nature of the dynamic interaction between these dimensions and the lower three would suggest the unlikelihood of an instantaneous and scientifically inexplicable starting point for the universe such as a divine miracle or a random quantum fluctuation occurring at a particular point.[18] Similarly, the endless source of matter and energy proposed by the writers suggests the possibility that the universe had no temporal beginning, and that there is no scientific reason for it to come to an end at some future point in time. A universe with the power to perpetuate itself indefinitely has no need of an all-powerful being to explain the creative process, or of a God who brings everything into being out of nothing.[19]

We will now examine the nature of the universe to discover whether it actually consists of matter, or whether it can be regarded as fundamentally non-physical.

1 William R. Corliss, "Quantum mechanics is definitely spooky," *Science Frontiers No. 114,* (Nov–Dec 1997).

2 See discussion below on string theory. The term "higher" is normally used to describe a dimension or dimensions beyond the three we know, though the concepts of "high" and "low" have no real meaning in this context.

3 Robert Nadeau and Menas Kafatos, *The Non-Local Universe: The New Physics and Matters of the Mind,* (Oxford: Oxford University Press, 1999), 4.

4 In 2011, Pope Benedict XVI stated that there was no incompatibility between religious faith and the Big Bang. See Russ Breighner, *Genesis, Faith, Science,* (Pittsburgh, PA: Dorrance Publishing Co. Inc., 2012), iii. For a discussion on the significance of the Big Bang among Muslim scholars,

see C.A.O. Van Nieuwenhuijze, "Religion versus Science in Islam: A Past and Future Question," *Die Welt des Islams*, New Series, 33, 2, (1993), 279.

5 Edwin Hubble, "A Relation between Distance and Radial Velocity among Extra-Galactic Nebulae," *Proceedings of the National Academy of Sciences of the United States of America* 15, 3 (1929), 168–173.

6 A random quantum fluctuation is a temporary change in the amount of energy in a point in space that allows for the creation of virtual particles and ultimately matter. Although this kind of fluctuation is a recognised feature of quantum mechanics, there is no explanation as to how it could have been the causal factor in the origins of the universe.

7 Michael S. Turner, "Cosmology Solved? Quite Possibly!", *Publications of the Astronomical Society of the Pacific*, Vol. 111, No. 757 (March 1999), 265.

8 In Einstein's general theory of relativity (1916), space is described as curved.

9 See discussion below on string theory.

10 Wikipedians, *Superstrings, P-branes and M theory: Theories of Everything*, (Mainz, Germany: PediaPress, 2011), 485.

11 In most of the works cited below, the authors provide some of the scientific data and mathematical calculations on which their theories are based.

12 Paul J. Steinhardt and Neil Turok, *Endless Universe: Beyond the Big Bang – Rewriting Cosmic History*, (New York: Broadway Books, 2007).

13 Paul A. LaViolette, *Subquantum Kinetics: A Systems Approach*, (Niskayuna, NY: Starlane Publications, 2010). Pages 299 to 307 provide a list of predictions made by the author that have subsequently been confirmed.

14 Manjir Samanta-Laughton, *Punk Science: Inside the Mind of God*, (Winchester, UK: O Books, 2006), Ch. 12.

15 The author accepts Einstein's view that the fourth

dimension is time, which would mean that she regards *c2* as the fifth dimension. Opinion generally seems to be divided on whether the fourth dimension represents time, or is a combination of time and space. String theorists generally associate time with the eleventh dimension.

16 David Bohm and Basil J. Hiley, *The Undivided Universe: An Ontological Interpretation of Quantum Theory,* London, Routledge, 1993), Ch. 15. Also see David Bohm, *Wholeness and the Implicate* Order, (New York: Routledge, 1980).

17 Renée Weber, "Field Consciousness and Field Ethics," *Re-Vision,* Summer/Fall 1978, 19.

18 See note 6.

19 As creatures of a three-dimensional world, we find it difficult to imagine that matter has always existed, and that there is no point at which we can mark the beginning of time. These limitations in our thought process have led to the idea of a mysterious God who is somehow "outside" time and space, which means there could be no beginning to his existence.

Chapter 9

Consciousness

The question as to whether a personal Creator is required to explain the origins and functioning of the universe, can be addressed firstly by defining the meaning of "universe." Sir Isaac Newton described it as a vast machine obeying mechanical laws, but more recently it has been understood as the totality of space-time, energy and matter. The accepted view that the scientist is distinct from the experimental material was disrupted with the advent of quantum theory, so that the mind of the observer is now regarded as being integral to the experimental process. It has also been shown that matter is able to follow principles. On those grounds it has been described as being "permeated by a conceptual level of existence,"[1] and the claim has been made that in the unfolding of physical reality, consciousness has a significant role to play.[2]

Historically, the relationship between matter and consciousness has been of interest to both philosophers and scientists. Particular attention is given to the manner in which the neurons in our brain are connected to the experiences of thinking and feeling. In the seventeenth century, René Descartes described matter as a substance occupying space, and he saw the mind as a thinking substance that has no location. After pointing out that the mind and the body are involved in both voluntary movement and the experience of sensation, he suggested that it is God who ensures that the union between the mental and the physical is preserved.[3] While rejecting such a role for the divine, some scientists retain the view that consciousness and matter are mutually exclusive concepts. Others have proposed a chain of causes, beginning with elementary particles, followed by atoms, molecules, neurons and ultimately the brain as a whole.

Consciousness is thereby depicted as a product of the brain.[4] An alternative approach involves reducing everything to the physical, so that all reality, including consciousness, is held to consist merely of material interactions.[5]

Both the ideas of Descartes, and theories where everything is regarded as material, are rejected by Daniel Dennett. He nevertheless describes human consciousness as a "virtual machine,"[6] or an "evolving computer program that shapes the activities of the brain." Dennett proposes an analogy between the gradual evolution of biological species and the emergence of conscious thoughts. We cannot locate a particular species or a thought in a given time or place, each evolutionary event being situated in a wider process based on the dynamic organization of sub-events. In a similar manner, the biologists Francis Crick and Christof Koch suggest that the mind emerges when a given level of complexity is reached, and that consciousness may be the outcome when certain neurons oscillate coherently.[7] They apply this view to the evolution of the human species in terms of the first appearance of a mind. Approaches such as these represent an attempt to undermine Descartes' view of the absolute separation between mind and matter.

A further departure from Descartes comes from theorists who regard consciousness as the fundamental reality. Galen Strawson challenges conceptual schemes that begin by describing physical matter as non-conscious and non-experiential, and then claim that "when parts of it combine in certain ways, experiential phenomena 'emerge.'"[8] Strawson's position is that if Y emerges from X, Y must be wholly dependent on X, and that all the features of Y must be traceable back to X. Through the application of this principle, Strawson concludes that the origin of human consciousness must be experiential in its basic nature.[9] He claims that some thinkers are so committed to the irreconcilability of the experiential and the physical that they effectively deny the former. The development of this kind of approach is described by Strawson as "the strangest thing that has ever happened in the whole history of human thought."[10] Catherine Roberts suggests that for many scientists, the notion that the evolutionary process culminated in the vast intellectual powers of the human mind is regarded simply as a happy, fortuitous development in a world of purposeless matter obeying physical and chemical laws.[11]

From an evolutionary viewpoint, Sewall Wright contends that there is no scientific explanation for the emergence of mind from matter, and that mind must have already been present when life arose.[12] Such a view is reflected in Colin McGinn's claim that "a supernatural magician" would be required to derive sentience and consciousness from what he calls "pulpy matter."[13] The physicist Paul Davies also challenges the idea that the characteristic features of consciousness are a product of the evolutionary process. His position is that a universal mind pervades the cosmos. Describing this mind as "a self-observing as well as self-organizing system,"[14] he suggests that individual minds can be regarded as "'islands' of consciousness in a sea of mind." Max Planck, a major figure in the development of quantum theory, claims that matter derives from consciousness, which in his view is the fundamental reality.[15]

Certain theorists in the field of biology have similarly argued for the inseparability of mind and matter. They claim that a primitive form of consciousness can be seen in the activity of the cell, where a DNA molecule copies itself to produce two identical molecules. Through the ongoing process of cell division, the various organs of the body are formed.[16] Cells somehow "know" how to differentiate and to pass the required information to subsequent cells. Yet scientists who adopt the traditional view cannot explain how these processes are accomplished.[17] A single bacterial cell, which is the smallest unit of life, has a structure that is more complex than anything else that has been discovered in the universe.[18] In response to the Newtonian view that the whole of any object is merely the sum of its constituent parts, Arthur Zajonc points out that the development of the embryo does not involve an addition of one cell to another so as to form a foetus. It is rather the case that even the first cell has a structure that determines the way a physical form will develop.[19] According to the biologist Charles Birch, brain cells are sentient, and that as a general principle of nature "things that feel are made of things that feel."[20]

One of the difficulties in attempts to divide reality into the conscious and non-conscious lies in establishing where the boundary lies between the two. Stanley Sobottka asks: "If mammals are conscious, are birds? Are insects? What about amoebas and bacteria? [...] If complexity is the only criterion for consciousness, what about inanimate objects? If they are included, at what level of complexity? If they are excluded, why are they excluded?"[21] The same kind of problem is addressed by David Pratt in discussing how to delineate the living from the non-living. He suggests that if the criterion for life is the exchange of matter and energy with the surroundings, all natural systems would have to be included.[22] Neither life nor consciousness could therefore be regarded as self-contained concepts.

Thinkers in various disciplines hold the view that a mysterious realm of potentiality is the source of consciousness in its various expressions, including that of matter, animals, humans, and the physical universe itself.[23] Recent research indicates that the development of multicellular animals such as human beings is made possible through a capacity that is already possessed by more primitive organisms such as single-cell amoebas.[24] If the realm of potentiality is understood as multidimensional, consciousness would be manifest in differing ways in these various dimensions. Primitive forms such as particles would exhibit a primitive form of consciousness. Particles with a dimension of zero or one would be less complex than particles with two dimensions, and the latter in turn would be less complex than particles with three dimensions. This progression would involve a corresponding development in the respective levels of consciousness. Samanta-Laughton writes, "It is consciousness itself that undergoes evolution and this is reflected in the increasing complexity of species."[25]

Among quantum physicists there is an increasing awareness that the material they are working with contains evidence of "subjective" characteristics such as intelligence and self-awareness. The fact that particles in an experiment change their physical status as a result of being observed, indicates that they have a sensitivity to their environment that is not apparent in our everyday experience of physical objects. Based on the evidence of consciousness in the decisions made by particles between alternative possibilities, Freeman Dyson asserts that mind and knowing are universal in nature.[26] In support of this position, Basil Hiley suggests that there is merely a difference in degree rather than in kind between the human act of choosing and that exhibited by particles.[27]

The work of David Bohm discusses an invisible enfolded implicate order that continually unfolds as the three-dimensional explicate order. Describing the implicate order as a form of consciousness that can be understood as a series of moments, he writes: "One moment gives rise to the next, in which context that was previously implicate is now explicate while the previous explicate content has become implicate."[28] Consciousness is a feedback process that results in a progressive accumulation of understanding. In the undivided wholeness of the implicate order, everything is continually forming and dissolving, consciousness and matter being different aspects of this unbroken movement.[29] According to Bohm, the deepest aspect of being is "neither mind nor body but rather a yet higher-dimensional actuality"[30] in which these two aspects of existence are united. Any attempt to divide the universe into living and nonliving things is meaningless. For Bohm, "even a rock is in some way alive, for life and intelligence are present not only in all of matter, but in energy, space, time, the fabric of the entire universe... Everything is alive. What we call dead is an abstraction."[31] Bohm's position is that consciousness is present in a rudimentary form for particles, and at a higher level for us. In his view, we are an intrinsic part of the universe, and our participation in the whole of reality gives it meaning. Because of this mutual involvement, the implicate order grows in its understanding and self-awareness.[32] Joseph Jaworski writes, "In discovering our own purpose and meaning, we enrich meaning in the universe – we create something of significance that has not been there. We are part of it and it is part of us. *We are partners in the evolution of the universe.*"[33]

In modern Western thought, the scientific understanding of the universe as conscious has arisen mainly as a result of quantum discoveries. The writers of the sacred texts obviously did not have access to such information, with the result that theists as a whole have been reluctant to accept the idea that matter is conscious. Instead, they rely on the biblical account that God formed from dust the first man, Adam, and then gave him the breath of life.[34] Consciousness or life is thereby seen as a gift that is bestowed on human beings, with matter itself remaining lifeless.

The idea that the universe is conscious creates problems both for believers in a personal God and for those who deny the existence of the divine.[35] As David Ash explains:

> Theists may assume the Universe is inanimate material in motion created by a prime mover and atheists may argue there is no Creator or prime mover of the presumed material. However, if the Universe is mind there would be no material to move and no prime mover to move it. The very nature of mind is creative consciousness. One wouldn't need to imagine an intelligent being creating the Universe if the

> Universe is a mind. The Universe would be the intelligent being! To know the mind of God is to know the Universe of energy and that is what science is all about.[36]

Groups of people within the religious traditions have had experiences that suggest the existence of a dimension transcending the limitations of our normal thought processes. We will now examine these experiences and the effect they have had, both on the individuals concerned, and on the traditions to which they have given allegiance.

1 Attila Grandpierre, "Ultimate Reality and Meaning," *The Noetic Journal*, 23, 12–35 (2000), *www.mindspring.com/~noeticj*
2 Henry P. Stapp, "Why Classical Mechanics Cannot Naturally Accommodate Consciousness But Quantum Mechanics Can," *http://arxiv.org/pdf/quant-ph/9502012vl.pdf*, 2008.
3 Descartes, *Principles of Philosophy*, tr. V. R. Miller and R.P. Miller (Dordrecht: Reidel, 1983); I:51 (original Latin publication 1644).
4 Amit Goswami, "Physics within Nondual Consciousness," *Philosophy East and West*, 51, 4, 536.
5 Paavo Pylkkkänen, *Mind, Matter, and the Implicate Order*, (New York: Springer, 2007), 6.
6 Daniel C. Dennett, *Consciousness Explained*, (Boston: Little, Brown and Company, 1991), 431.
7 David Chalmers, "The Puzzle of Conscious Experience," *Scientific American*, 273 (1995), 80–86.
8 Galen Strawson, "Realistic monism: why physicalism entails panpsychism," *Journal of Consciousness Studies*,13, 10–11, 2006.
9 Ibid.
10 Ibid.
11 Catherine Roberts, "Insight in Science and in Plato," *Manas*

Journal, xxxvi, 9, (1983), 2.

12 Sewald Wright, "Panpsychism and Science," in J.B. Cobb and D.R. Griffin (eds.), *Mind in Nature: Essays on the Interface of Science and Philosophy* (Lanham, MD: University Press of America, 1977), 82.

13 Colin McGinn, *The Problem of Consciousness: Essays Toward a Resolution*, (Malden, MA: Blackwell, 1991), 45.

14 Paul Davies, *God and the New Physics*, (London: Penguin Books Ltd., 1983), 210.

15 Max Planck, *The Observer*, January 25, 1931.

16 A cell in biology is the basic unit that contains the fundamental molecules of life. Some cells acquire specialized functions and co-operate with other specialized cells, eventually forming large multicellular organisms such as animals and humans.

17 Lynne McTaggart, *The Field: The Quest for the Secret Force of the Universe*, (London: HarperCollins, 2009), 46.

18 Lynn Margulis and Dorian Sagan, *Microcosmos: Four Billion Years from Our Microbial Ancestors* (New York: Simon & Schuster, 1986), 35.

19 Arthur Zajonc, "New Wine in What Kind of Wineskins? Metaphysics in the Twenty-First Century," in Willis Harman and Jane Clark (eds.), *New Metaphysical Foundations of Modern Science*, (Sausalito, CA: Institute of Noetic Sciences, 1994), 322.

20 Charles Birch, *On Purpose* (Sydney: New South Wales University Press, 1990), 33.

21 Stanley Sobottka, "The three major metaphysical philosophies," (Charlottesville, VA: University of Virginia, 2010), *faculty.virginia.edu/consciousness/new_page_4.htm*.

22 David Pratt, "The Monistic Idealism of A. Goswami," *davidpratt.info/goswami.htm*.

23 This realm of potentiality is addressed in the work of David Bohm discussed below, and also in the philosophies of

Plato, Heidegger and Deleuze. See Ch. 6.

24 "Primitive forms of complex human processes identified in Amoeba," *Phys.org,* Feb 22, 2013. See also M. Clarke and A. Lohan et al., *Genome Biology*, 2013, 14: R11.

25 Samanta-Laughton, 2006, 64.

26 Freeman Dyson, *Infinite in All Directions*, (New York: Harper & Row, 1988), 297.

27 Basil J. Hiley, "Process and the Implicate Order: their relevance to Quantum Theory and Mind," *http://www.ctr4process.org/publications/Articles/LSI05/Hiley%20paper.pdf*, 2.

28 David Bohm, *Wholeness and the Implicate Order*, (London: Routledge & Kegan Paul, 1980), 260.

29 Ibid., 11.

30 Ibid., 209.

31 Renée Weber, *Dialogues with Scientists and Sages*, (London: Routledge & Kegan Paul, 1986).

32 Beatrix Murrell, "The Cosmic Plenum: Bohm's Gnosis: The Implicate Order," *www.bizcharts.com/stoa_del_sol/plenum/plenum_3.html*.

33 Joseph Jaworski, *Source: The Inner Path of Knowing Creation* (San Francisco: Berrett-Koehler Publishers, Inc., 2012), 96.

34 Genesis 2:7.

35 An alternative that has been proposed to the idea of a personal God is that the deity is the "ground of being." See Paul Tillich, *Systematic Theology*, Vol. 1, (Chicago: University of Chicago Press, 2012), 64. If the universe is regarded merely as space, energy, and matter, it is reasonable to suppose that something or someone else is required to explain the whole. But if the universe is conscious, and if it has always existed, the universe would be its own ground of being.

36 David Ash, *Vortex of Energy: A Scientific Theory*, (Berkshire, UK: Puja Power Publications, 2012), 127.

Chapter 10

Participation in the Divine

The idea that the whole of reality is ultimately one presents challenges to the commonly held view that we are self-contained individuals, separate from each other and from the physical world, and to the belief that the disparate properties of the mental and the physical indicate that each is irreducible to the other. Descartes' theory that God is involved in the interaction between the mind and the body, is supported in the thought of Newton, who writes that through the creative acts of God, bodies are able to combine with minds, while being distinct from them.[1] Theists believe that in his act of creation, God made human beings in his own image, and gave them control over the physical world.[2] Because of this "delegated" authority,[3] the kind of gulf that exists between God and the material order is assumed to be partially reflected in the relationship between humanity and the natural world.

In what is known as modern classical science,[4] everything is determined against a background of absolute space and time, and scientific theory is held to be a precise representation of reality.[5] Scientists are seen as the subjects and the experimental materials are the objects. Before the advent of quantum theory, there seemed to be no reason for belief in any form of underlying oneness. With the challenges to this view arising from discoveries in the twentieth century, the interconnection that was found to exist between all aspects of reality has led to a renewed appraisal of the alleged distance between the Creator, human beings, and the physical universe.

An earlier chapter outlined the experiences of mystics, where everything seems to be absorbed into a mysterious unity.[6] While it is quite possible for a person without religious beliefs to have such an experience, many who engage in these practices have previously embraced the idea of a personal God who brought everything into being. The experiences themselves, however, can be so overwhelming that in the interpretation that may occur after the event, the idea of an all-powerful, transcendent God is replaced with a form of reality where no fundamental division exists—either between a Creator and his creation, or between conscious beings and seemingly inanimate matter. An alternative response involves the attempt to reconcile the nature of the experience with the traditional view of a God who transcends all reality. The result in these cases is often a diminution of the idea of oneness in favor of the accepted doctrine. With regard to those individuals who already consider the gulf between the infinite, perfect God and finite, sinful human beings to be unbridgeable, the strength of their conviction may effectively preclude them from being able to enter into the ultimate experience of union.

In each of the monotheisms, a tradition of mystical ideas emphasising the oneness of all reality has been in tension with the established doctrines proclaimed by religious authorities. Although it cannot be proved that truth lies within the domain of the mystical rather than within orthodox teachings, the similarities between the interpretation of mystical experiences and recent discoveries in science suggest the possibility that while coming from differing perspectives, each approach is pointing to the same ultimate reality that is beyond our immediate comprehension.

Theism and the mystics

A fundamental doctrine in the religious traditions is that our estrangement from God is caused by our sinfulness and disobedience to his commands. The Hebrew scriptures depict God's view of his creatures: "The Lord looks down from heaven on all mankind to see if any act wisely, if any seek out God. But all are disloyal, all are rotten to the core."[7] The idea of universal human depravity is carried over into Christianity, where St. Paul endorses the above verse from the Psalms.[8] But whereas in Hebrew teaching, people could have a relationship with God by offering sacrifices and striving to keep his commandments, in Christianity the evil of humans is so extreme that only the death of God's son can save them. Furthermore, in both Christianity and Islam, Hell is described as a place of eternal punishment for those who refuse to believe in God.[9]

Whenever new religions are formed, their founders and some of their early followers are likely to have had experiences that are mystical or in other ways are life-transforming. Such experiences form the basis of subsequent beliefs and behavior.[10] For example, as a result of the revelations he received, the Prophet Muhammad decreed that the rich must accept responsibility for helping the poor and the dispossessed.[11] Within each of the traditions, the dissemination of the various teachings eventually resulted in the establishment of religious institutions. Power fell into the hands of a few, who claimed the right to determine "correct" teachings and to decree the eternal fate of nonbelievers.

In his overview of early church history, Don Cupitt writes that after a period of time following the death of Jesus, "the religious professionals ... monopolized control of the sacred text, worship, doctrine, preaching, and religious law."[12] Under what he describes as "a large and bureaucratic salvation-machine," the possibility that individuals could have a direct personal experience of religious happiness and liberation was strongly resisted. In its place was the teaching that if people were submissive to the religious leaders in all matters of faith and practice, they would experience happiness, but only after death. William James comments that "when a religion has become an orthodoxy, its day of inwardness is over; the spring is dry." He describes this as a process that involves a stifling of the "spontaneous religious spirit."[13] From the time the early church became a hierarchical structure, individuals' experiences that seemed to run counter to the approved teachings were condemned as heresy.

An area of concern to religious authorities generally was the claim by certain of their adherents that through their mystical experiences they were already participating in divinity, or that they had the capacity to become one with the divine.[14] Such claims were resisted on the grounds that sinful human beings could never be a part of divinity. In each of the monotheisms it is believed that God's will and purposes have been revealed to one or more selected individuals, and that the relevant teachings have been maintained either through the written word or by means of a historical tradition whereby the divine truth has been preserved. These teachings are claimed to be binding on the whole of humanity. For example, the Hebrew scriptures depict cases where people who worshipped other gods and refused to obey the one true God were killed at his command.[15]

Absolute faith in the historical purity of their belief system has led religious leaders at various times to denounce those who claimed to have had private experiences of exaltation, and even to engage in the persecution of such individuals (see below). The lack of retaliation on the part of those who suffered in this way, when compared with the behavior of their persecutors, would suggest that whatever ultimate truth may be, it is more likely to be reflected in the interpretation of this kind of experience than in the punitive doctrines of orthodoxy. Within Christianity today, the passion with which certain of the more conservative elements claim an exclusive grasp of the truth, is a reflection of the statement made by St. Paul that if any person, or even an angel, were to deviate from the original teachings given to him by God, such an individual or entity should be accursed.[16]

Hebrew/Judaism

In the Hebrew/Jewish tradition, the source of mystical ideas is the Kabbalah. Its teachings were originally believed to have been given by God to Abraham and Moses, and then through David and Solomon in an oral tradition lasting until the destruction of the Second Temple in 70 CE. Following this event, a written scriptural commentary on the Kabbalah appeared called the Zohar. It was said to encapsulate the mind of God revealed in the Torah, which contains the five books of Moses and appears at the beginning of the Hebrew scriptures. From the fourteenth century onwards, the Zohar was accepted as the main text of the Kabbalah. Religious leaders at the time feared, however, that if ordinary people were given access to these writings, they could be misunderstood, so only learned scholars were permitted to read them.[17]

The deity is described in the Kabbalah as having two aspects: one is the absolute and limitless divine; the other is a manifestation through which God is revealed to his creatures. *Ein Sof* is the name given to God as the mysterious, infinite reality. This unknowable spiritual realm "descends" to create a physical counterpart of itself as the world we know, in a continuous process of emergence, evolvement and transformation.[18] An authoritative exposition of the sacred texts was given by Isaac Luria (1534–1572), who was both a rabbi and a mystic. In what became known as the Lurianic Kabbalah, God is described as filling everything with his presence, including human beings. Luria writes that God "contracted" his infinite light so as to allow the formation of an independent realm carrying sparks of divinity, and that through these inner manifestations, we are able to know the Creator.[19]

Traditional Judaism adopted some of the above teachings, but it added ascetic practices such as fasting, penance, and self-mortification,[20] together with warnings of Heaven and Hell. These ideas, in combination with a legalistic formalism, were seen by certain groups as being far removed from genuine religious experience. In the eighteenth century, a rabbi in Eastern Europe, Israel Baal Shem Tov, presented an alternative system of thought and practice that became known as Hasidism. Whereas Luria's teaching includes the idea of a transcendent God, Shem Tov focused on the presence of the immanent divine in everything.[21] He distinguished between the Kabbalah as a text that can be learned by anyone, and the experience of oneness that is beyond our intellectual comprehension. This kind of mystical union forms a link between God and creation. When human beings look at material things, they are actually gazing at the image of the deity, since the whole of creation is infused with the divine.[22] For Shem Tov "nothing exists in this world except the Absolute Unity which is God."[23]

The quest of the Hasidists was to penetrate into the inner depths of the biblical account, and they did so by "reintroducing into Judaism the mythical and pantheistic dimensions of the life of the spirit."[24] From early in its history until the nineteenth century, there was strong opposition to Hasidism, and its followers suffered bitter persecution by the religious authorities.[25] In parts of Europe, the Hasidists were excommunicated from the believing community. They were also denounced to the authorities as traitors, as a result of which some of them were imprisoned. For the traditionalists, the major problem with Hasidic teaching was its belief in the identity of the universe and the divine.

Christianity

Following the death of Jesus, various manuscripts were in existence outlining the events of his life and teaching. What followed was the compiling of the scriptural canon in the fourth century. The main reason for this length of time was the existence of a wide variety of ideas regarding who Jesus was, and the nature of his purposes in the lives of his followers.[26]

By the end of the second century, what eventually became the official church had become a hierarchical institution of bishops, priests, and deacons. Creeds and doctrines were formulated, and no deviation from authorized teachings was permitted.

An alternative approach to sacred truth that ran concurrently with the official view was outlined in ancient texts discovered in upper Egypt in 1945, where they had been concealed inside a cave. These writings, known as the Nag Hammadi Library, contain gospels that describe Jesus' life, and at least one of the authors was among the original group of his disciples.[27] Some scholars consider that the Gospel of Thomas, dating from the first century CE, is among the first of such accounts to be written.[28] It includes material recorded in the biblical gospels. The focus of this teaching is the possibility of becoming one with the divine. Today these writers are referred to as Gnostics—a term derived from the Greek word *gnosis,* which is the kind of knowledge gained through direct spiritual insight. The mystical ideas held by the Gnostics were influenced by pre-Christian thinkers such as Philo of Alexandria, who had produced a synthesis of Greek and Hebrew thought. On the question of who Jesus was, the orthodox position identified him as God in human form, whereas for the Gnostics, Jesus was not God, but one who taught about the divine light within us all.[29] He demonstrated this kind of life so that we could follow his example.

A central teaching of Gnosticism is that to know the self at the deepest level is to know God, as indicated in the statement, "Look for God by taking yourself as the starting point."[30] A second-century Gnostic, Marcus, believed that everyone was part of the same whole, and that this oneness will be restored when we choose to see past the illusion of separation.[31] For the Gnostics, our true home is a realm of light—a place outside matter. They taught that we are multidimensional beings and are connected to the universe, which contains parallel dimensions beyond the three we know.[32] Upon our original descent into mortality, we left behind our divine image, forgetting our true origin. The task we now have is to find our way back to the realm of light so as to be reunited with God. Because we are of divine origin, we can pursue this goal in our earthly lives through a union with the "divine spark," or the God within us. Whereas believers within the church had to exercise faith in a supernatural being, as taught by the religious authorities, Gnostics believed they had evolved beyond that level by connecting with their inner light. In the Gospel of Thomas, Jesus says, "There is a light within each person, and it lights up the whole universe."[33] Lee Hager suggests that for Gnostics, God is not an entity outside the universe, nor is God's kingdom "a place or a thing" but rather a spiritual reality permeating everything in existence.[34]

One of the teachings of Gnosticism concerned the question of creation. Together with many other groups within the early Christian community, Gnostics held that everything is an emanation from the one eternal source, and that the human soul in itself is spiritual and immortal. Against this view, the traditionalists argued that "man could not be on a par with God ... therefore his soul could not be part of God. It could not have been created out of God's essence. God must have created souls—along with bodies and the rest of the material universe—out of nothing at all."[35]

As the ultimate authorities on doctrine, the early church fathers sought to discredit the Gnostics by portraying their ideas as absurd and misguided, and casting false aspersions on their moral behavior.[36] In commenting on reactions to mystical writing, Cupitt explains how dangerous these ideas can be in any age: "Religious authorities are always very alert and quick to detect an implicit criticism of themselves and a threat to their power and privileges."[37] After a period of time, Gnosticism was declared a heresy and its members were persecuted by the church, many of them being tortured and put to death. Most of their writings were destroyed. Official teaching was based on the idea that salvation belonged to the church and its sacraments, and could never depend on an individual's personal experience. When the Roman emperor, Constantine I, declared Christianity to be the state religion in the fourth century, the killing of Gnostics was officially sanctioned on the grounds that they were potential enemies of the social order. But the most powerful motivation for these punitive acts was the belief that through his servants, God was visiting judgment upon his enemies—those who held different ideas from the doctrines proclaimed by the church. Such individuals were later described as worse than pagans, Muslims or Jews, since they had "betrayed Christ."[38]

The medieval period witnessed a growth in mysticism, where the authoritarian structures of the church were bypassed in favor of personal spiritual journeys.[39] As long as individuals recognised the gulf separating them from God, no action was taken by the authorities. But for those who claimed to have experienced some kind of identity with the divine, excommunication or legal action could ensue. Even the great theologian and mystic Meister Eckhart was tried for heresy by Pope John XXII in the fourteenth century. The writings on which he was condemned included statements such as, "God must be very I, I very God, so consummately one that this he and this I are one 'is.'"[40]

Islam

The Muslim tradition was founded by the Prophet Muhammad early in the seventh century, when he received revelations from God (Allah) that subsequently became the Quran. Sufism, the main mystical movement within Islam, arose in the eighth century. In its early stages, the Sufis were influenced by the austere practices of groups known as ascetics, some of whom were friends of the Prophet. During that period, Muhammad's followers divided into two groups: one comprised the theologians and jurists; the other consisted of people whose focus was on personal religious devotion. The former group developed into a powerful institution, while the Sufis saw problems in its purely intellectual approach and the prominence given to the observance of rules.[41]

Within Sufism, ascetic practices were later replaced by mystical experiences of oneness with God. In an attempt to show the continuity of their ideas with those of the tradition, the Sufis made increasing reference to the Quran and statements of Muhammad.[42] Whereas the Islamic authorities regarded the revelation given to the Prophet as complete, Sufis rejected the idea of fixed doctrine. They allowed themselves to be open to the possibility of new experiences, finding wisdom in religions such as Christianity. The true foundation of Islamic law, as Sufis understood it, was the interior life of its founder. They therefore sought to have the kinds of experiences that had enabled the Quranic revelations to be received by the Prophet, whom they regarded as the original Sufi master. The overall goal for Sufis is to be absorbed in God, since he is the ground of all being. Everything that exists is therefore an aspect of divine reality. While Muslims are obliged to believe that there is no reality but God, the Sufis take this to mean that if God alone is real, God alone *is.* They hold that "in the Absolute Oneness there is no separate polarity between Subject and Object, between knower and known. To be known by God is thus, mysteriously, to be God."[43] Sufis describe a vision involving a loss of personal identity and a fusion with the divine.

The seventeenth-century thinker Ahmad Sirhindi contested the Sufist interpretation by claiming that everything merely comes from God,[44] and that whatever we know is a mere shadow of that ultimate reality. Any experience suggesting a union between God and the world, or between God and human beings, can never be regarded as objective truth. The reality of God transcends the universe and all it contains. Other Islamic commentators suggested that the mystical state should be understood simply as a cognitive unity characterised by the loss of the consciousness of selfhood. But for many who undergo the experience, it is felt as a unity of substance, or a genuine identity between the human and the divine. The twelfth-century scholar Abu Hamid al-Ghazali speaks of an "annihilation in unity," where the mystic "sees nothing in the world save the One ... and thereby does not even see himself insofar as he is thoroughly engrossed in unity."[45]

A writer who had a considerable influence on the development of Sufist thought was Ibn al-Arabi, who died in 1240. He claimed that being and existence are combined in God, and that prior to the creation of individual things and beings, everything was one with the divine.[46] This mysterious deity was interpreted by al-Arabi as an undifferentiated unity containing the archetypes of all potential beings. It was also seen as the "supreme reality" that is expressed in two forms: one is hidden and indeterminate; the other is manifest through created things that are identical with it.[47] For al-Arabi, the process of creation is a "sacred effusion"—an overflowing or emanation of the divine.[48]

Sufis who experience identity with the Absolute Being describe passing through a stage of accepting the basic creed that there is no god but Allah, then to a second stage where they are able to say, "There is no god but Thou," and to the final stage where they proclaim, "There is no god but I."[49] The tenth-century mystic and poet al-Hallaj claimed to have experienced such a union. He is reported to have said "I am the Truth," indicating that he saw himself as divine. This position was further revealed in a piece of his writing: "I am He whom I love, and He whom I love is I: We are two spirits dwelling in one body. If thou seest me thou seest Him, And if thou seest Him thou seest us both."[50] Statements such as these enraged the authorities, and after al-Hallaj had been imprisoned for eleven years, he was brutally tortured to death. Today Sufis accept the union of the human and the divine, since they regard it as "the Supreme Truth and therefore the ultimate goal of all mysticism."[51]

Reinterpreting the divine

Within the monotheistic traditions, mystics in every era have generally portrayed themselves as holding to the idea of a personal deity, partly because such a belief would normally have formed part of their upbringing, and partly through their fear of rejection or persecution at the hands of religious authorities. But by positing an unknowable divinity such as the *Ein Sof* in the Kabbalah, or the "God beyond God" in the thought of Meister Eckhart, mystics can acknowledge the existence of a divine being, while holding that such a deity does not have the status accorded to him in the traditions. From a mystical perspective, the doctrine of a personal divinity reflects the limitations of human thought in the various attempts that have been made to comprehend the mystery of undifferentiated oneness. The accounts given by mystics can include a feeling that "there is no reporter and no observed content. There is only the massive all-encompassing presence of the One."[52] Mystics sometimes interpret their experience as an effusion or emanation, where the individual expresses the spirituality and immortality that in orthodox teaching is reserved for the deity.

The accounts given by mystics are consistent with the scientific view that matter and thought arise from an indivisible wholeness, and that the self-contained identity commonly attributed to beings and objects merely reflects our limited understanding as creatures living in a three-dimensional world. In contrast to the modern classical idea of the separateness between ourselves and everything else, Bohm and Hiley suggest that each of the unfolded elements in the explicate order—the world we know, is a particular manifestation of the totality—the implicate order. The process of enfolding into the implicate order where everything is one, and unfolding out of it into individual forms, has been linked to the concept of the spreading wave that can appear as a particle in a certain location, only to be reabsorbed into a dimension beyond the visible universe. Similarly in the interpretations of mystical experience, each expression of matter and mind is regarded as a unique reflection of ultimate reality.

In the development of quantum theory, the instantaneous communication found to exist between seemingly distant particles suggested the likelihood of higher dimensions beyond the three of our everyday existence. Some string theorists hold to the view that the higher dimensions have higher vibrating frequencies than our own. According to Peter Rogers, humans are multidimensional beings, but that because we are limited by our three-dimensional bodies, under normal circumstances we are unable to experience the dimensions that vibrate at a faster rate.[53] Should mystical experience involve access to a dimension transcending space and time, it would be expected that mystics would lose any sense of space as we know it, so that nothing would be experienced as being closer or further away. Similarly with regard to time, there would be no experience of sequentiality. Mystics commonly report that they lacked any awareness of distance or directionality, and that they had no sense of one impression being followed by another. Many of the subjects in research conducted by Abraham Maslow describe either a "disorientation in time and space" or "the lack of consciousness of time and space."[54]

If the conscious universe is the source of all reality, it could in some sense be regarded as divine. But if each individual is a unique expression of that totality, and is both a participator in, and a contributor to, the experience of the cosmos,[55] there would seem to be no place for a transcendent God, in particular, one who is angry with our rebellion against him, but yet will forgive our sins. The alternative view—that there is no supreme being but that we are each a unique expression of the divine—would suggest that the only forgiveness that would ever be necessary is that which we give to ourselves and, where appropriate, to others.

It is also claimed in the monotheisms that God continually demonstrates his love towards us. Apart from the fact that this God is said to punish those who reject the very idea of his existence, the believer will always be held to account for behavior that does not measure up to the divine standard of perfection. As a result, most committed believers will readily admit to numerous shortcomings. While it is one thing to acknowledge and accept responsibility for behavior we may have reason to regret, the possibility of being judged by a perfect God stands in sharp contrast to the simple recognition that as fallible human beings, we will sometimes fall short in seeking to fulfill our potential. If there is no all-powerful being to whom we must give account, we can recognise that even the worst of our behavior forms part of the means by which we each, as unique expressions of the totality, can learn and grow.

In this section we have examined the scientific finding that the universe is an undivided whole, together with claims that it is conscious and that it may have always existed. It was also suggested that the experience of mystics involving the absence of awareness of the self or of identifiable beings or objects, serves to confirm the ultimate oneness of everything in existence. Furthermore, should it be scientifically established that the universe contains higher spatial dimensions, it is reasonable to conclude that human beings are integral to this multidimensional reality.

The next section will examine the implications of religious experience, both mystical and non-mystical, with regard to the complex relationship that exists between what we consciously accept as fact, and the way the deeper levels of our being respond to ideas that address our most fundamental needs.

1 A. Rupert Hall and Marie Boas Hall (eds.), *Unpublished Scientific Papers of Isaac Newton,* (Cambridge: Cambridge University Press, 1978), 142.
2 Genesis 1.
3 J. Rosalie Hooge, *Providential Beginnings,* (Maitland, FL: Xulon Press, 2003), 40.
4 Modern classical science refers to a period beginning in about the eighteenth century. It was an outcome of the high value placed on humans' reasoning ability by thinkers of the Enlightenment.
5 F. David Peat (ed.), *The Pari Dialogues: Essays in Science, Religion, Society and the Arts,* (Grosetto, Italy: Pari Publishing, 2007), 104.
6 See Chapter 4.
7 Psalm 14:2.
8 Romans 3: 10–12.
9 Luke 16: 23–24.
10 In this context, Abraham Maslow writes, "Much theology, much verbal religion through history and throughout the world, can be considered to be the more or less vain efforts to put into communicable words and formulae, and into symbolic rituals and ceremonies, the original mystical experience of the original prophets." Abraham H. Maslow, *Religions, Values, and Peak Experiences,* (London: Penguin Books, 1976).
11 Quran 22: 49–50.
12 Don Cupitt, *Mysticism after Modernity,*(Oxford: Blackwell, 1998), 3.
13 William James, *The Varieties of Religious Experience,* (Rockville, MD: Arc Manor, 2008), 249.
14 See examples given below of the persecution of mystics within Judaism, Christianity, and Islam.

15 See Joshua 8: 1–28, where God ordered that all the inhabitants of Ai were to be slain.

16 Galatians 1:8.

17 Edward Hoffman, *The way of splendor: Jewish Mysticism and Modern Psychology,* (Lanham, MD: Rowman & Littlefield Publishers Inc., 2007), 22–23.

18 Daniel C. Matt, *The Essential Kabbalah,* (San Francisco: Harper, 1995), 99.

19 Louis Jacobs, *A Jewish Theology,*(Springfield, NJ: Behrman House Inc., 1973), 32.

20 Mark J. Boda, Daniel K. Fork, and Rodney A. Werline (eds.), *Seeking the Favor of God: Volume 3, The Impact of Penitential Prayer beyond Second Temple Judaism,* (Atlanta GA: The Society of Biblical Literature, 2008), xi.

21 Martin Buber, *Hasidism and Modern Man,* (New York: Horizon Press, 1958), 187.

22 Norman Lamm, *The Religious Thought of Hasidism: Text and Commentary,* (Hoboken, NJ: KTAV Publishing House Inc., 1999), 49.

23 Jay Michaelson, *Everything Is God: The Radical Path of Nondual Judaism,* (Boston: Shambalah Publications Inc., 2009), 63.

24 Michael Oppenheim, "The Meaning of Hasidut: Martin Buber and Gershom Scholem," *Journal of the American Academy of Religion*, 49, 3, (1981), 417.

25 Maurice S. Friedman, *Martin Buber: The Life of Dialogue* (New York: Harpers, 1960), Ch. 3.

26 Elaine Pagels, *Beyond Belief: The Secret Gospel of Thomas* (New York: Random House, 2003), 32.

27 ___________, *The Gnostic Gospels,* (New York: Vintage Books, 1979), xiii–xxiii.

28 Stevan Davies, *The Gospel of Thomas: Annotated and Explained,* (Woodstock, VT: SkyLight Paths Publishing, 2003), xxii. For a discussion on the significance of the Gnostic Gospels, see John Dominic Crossan, "Foreword," in Hal Taussig (ed.), *A*

New New Testament: A Bible for the 21st Century Combining Traditional and Newly Discovered Texts, (Boston: Houghton Mifflin Harcourt, 2013).

29 Pagels (2003), 40.

30 Judith Anne Brown, *John Marco Allegro: The Maverick of the Dead Sea Scrolls,* (Michigan: W.B. Eerdmans Publishing Co., 2005), 254.

31 Lee Hager, "The Gnostic Gospels: A Bridge between Science and Spirituality" 2011, *www.selfgrowth.com*.

32 John V. Panella, *The Gnostic Papers: The Undiscovered Mysteries of Christ,* (Huntsville, AR: Ozark Mountain Publishers, 2002), 111.

33 Nag Hammadi Library 121, 24, cited in Pagels, 2003, op. cit., 56. (The English translation is by Pagels.)

34 Hager, (2011).

35 Phillip David, "The Wheel Broken at the Cistern: The Divergence of Orthodox Christianity from Gnosticism," *www.essene.com/EarlyChurch/OrthodoxFromGnostic*

36 Ibid., footnote 1: "The chief attacks on the Gnostics were authored by Church Fathers Irenaeus, Tertullian, and Epiphanius. But their work is seriously flawed and must be seen for what it is: religious polemic rather than history. Irenaeus, known as the First Church father, devoted five volumes to a work, *Adversus Haereses*, which purported to expose the Gnostics. Scholars have criticized it for its lack of objectivity and muddled thinking."

37 Cupitt, (1998), 4.

38 Jonathan Wright, *Heretics: The Creation of Christianity from the Gnostics to the Modern Church,* (New York: Houghton Mifflin Harcourt Publishing Company, 2011), 2.

39 See Chapter 4.

40 C. de B. Evans (tr.), *Meister Eckhart by Franz Pfeiffer,* (London: John M. Watkins, 1924), 247.

41 Karen Armstrong, *Islam: A Short History,* (New York: The

Modern Library, 2002), 74.

42 Fazlur Rahman, *Islam,* (London: University of Chicago press, 1979),134.

43 Martin Lings, *What Is Sufism?* (Berkeley: University of California Press, 1975), 65.

44 Annemarie Schimmel, *Islam in the Indian Subcontinent,* (Leiden, The Netherlands: E. J. Brill, 1980), 93.

45 Majid Fakhry, "Three Varieties of Mysticism in Islam," *International Journal for Philosophy of Religion,* 2, 4, (1971), 205.

46 Oliver Leaman (ed.), *Encyclopedia of Asian Philosophy,* (New York: Routledge, 2001), 74.

47 Fakhry, op. cit., 206.

48 Phyllis G. Jestice, *Holy People of the World: A Cross-Cultural Encyclopedia,* (Santa Barbara, CA: ABC–CLIO Inc., 2004), 386.

49 Steven Masood, "You + 1'd this publicly. *Wahdat al-Wujud*: a fundamental doctrine in Sufism,"www.stevenmasood.org/articles/Wahdat.html.

50 Karen Armstrong: *A History of God* (London: Vintage, 1999), 270.

51 Martin Lings, *A Sufi Saint of the Twentieth Century,* (London: George Allen & Unwin Ltd., 1971), 126.

52 Peter C. Appleby, "Mysticism and Ineffability," *International Journal for Philosophy of Religion,* 11, 3 (1980), 149.

53 Peter C. Rogers, *Universal Truth: Thinking outside the Box: Book II,* (Bloomington, IN: Author House, 2011), 282.

54 Maslow, op. cit.

55 See Chapter 9, endnote 34.

Section 3

God and Belief

Chapter 11

Exploring the Mind

The first section of this book discussed the thinking of some philosophers who use their differing experiences of the divine as a means of arguing for his existence. In the present section the question of the deity is addressed in the context of mystical and non-mystical religious experiences, and it analyzes the varying ways in which individuals are influenced in the conclusions they draw from these events. This chapter looks at mystical experiences from the point of view of the physiological changes involved, and examines the claims that have been made on the basis of the results obtained.

In recent years, investigations have been carried out on the brain processes of individuals while they were undergoing mystical experiences. A further type of study has involved the stimulation of a particular part of the brain, where the individual experiences the sense of a higher being. Findings from these kinds of research have been interpreted in differing ways. Some theorists hold that the altered brain patterns of the subjects indicate contact with a transcendent reality such as an all-powerful God, and that humans have been formed with the ability to communicate with this higher being. Opponents of this view argue that the results of the studies reveal nothing more than abnormal states of neural functioning.

To assess the implications of research into brain processes, it is useful to understand the way we give meaning to the information we receive from the outside world. This material is mediated through the five sensory systems.[1] Each of these systems has a primary receptive area, which receives the raw data and assembles it into a preliminary perception. For further refinement, the perception moves to the relevant secondary receptive area and then to the various association areas, where the information is integrated with data from the other senses. The association area involved with orientation has two sides: the left generates a mental sensation of a physically defined body, together with a spatial sense of difference between the self and the world; the right side orients the person with regard to the spatial relationship of the body to the objects in the environment. Abstract concepts and the comprehension and use of language are generated in the verbal conceptual association area, while the visual association area provides interpretations of perceptions and is also associated with memory. The attaining of goals involves the attention association area, which is concerned with concentration and contributes to the control of emotion. This area is also involved with beliefs, the will, habits of thought, personality development, self-awareness, memories and the generation of concepts.[2]

A recent development in the area of brain research into altered states of consciousness is that carried out by Andrew Newberg and his associates. From brain-imaging studies of Tibetan monks in a meditative state, and of Franciscan nuns at prayer, it was discovered that these practices involve the deprivation of sensory information to both sides of the orientation association area.[3] This kind of deprivation results in a sensation of spacelessness, and an absence of awareness of the boundaries between the self and the world. Furthermore, when there is a suspension of input to the areas of the brain associated with memory, hearing, and learning, there is no awareness of cause and effect, or of a before and an after. Everything exists in the moment.[4] Newberg writes, "The mind's perception of the self now becomes limitless; in fact there is no longer any sense of self at all. There would be no discrete objects or beings, no sense of space or the passage of time, no line between the 'self' and the rest of the universe – in fact there would be no subjective self at all – only an absolute sense of unity – without thought, without words, and without sensation."[5] This state is given the name "Absolute Unitary Being," and is described as "a state of pure awareness, a clear and vivid consciousness of nothing. Yet it is also a sudden, vivid consciousness of everything as an undifferentiated whole."[6] Such an experience is felt to be more real than both the external world and the subjective awareness of the self.[7] Newberg's basic position is that since both the experience of Absolute Unitary Being and the perception of objects are accompanied by changes in the brain, the former state should be understood as being just as real as the latter, and that mystical experiences support the idea of contact with a divine reality.

The idea that we can infer the existence of God through studies of the brain is contested by Jonathan Scott Miller, who argues that while the existence of a perceived object can be verified by independent observers, a similar process of verification would not be possible in respect of Absolute Unitary Being. For Miller, the experiences described should be seen merely as "occasions of sensory or cognitive impairment, and not of super-sensory contact,"[8] and that Newberg's position is weakened by his failure to address alternative explanations for the altered states of consciousness he discusses.

A further issue raised by Miller is that God is usually understood as a person—"a conscious being with thoughts and feelings,"[9] whereas the descriptions given of Absolute Unitary Being would suggest that such a concept could not fulfill the role of a God who loves and cares for his creatures. Matthew Ratcliffe points out that the monitoring of brain processes in general cannot establish the existence of any perceived object, and that this principle applies equally to the purported object of religious experiences.[10] Rather than providing a neural correlate to specific beliefs, studies of the brain can only investigate experiences in general. In Ratcliffe's view, the various aspects of religious belief and practice are inevitably influenced by the culture in which they are situated. Since belief systems differ in a variety of ways, the data from brain imaging studies would be inadequate to account for the full range of these experiences. In outlining the pervasive effects of culture on experience, Gregory Peterson explains that "Buddhist monks do not have visions of the virgin Mary and Catholic nuns do not go on vision quests."[11]

Newberg's approach is complicated by the fact that Absolute Unitary Being is sometimes portrayed merely as a state of individual consciousness, and at other times it is described as containing within itself the external world and subjective awareness, or even as being the Creator of both.[12] Although he has no doubt about the process of divine creation,[13] Newberg is unable to explain how Absolute Unitary Being could be synonymous with brain states, and at the same time be responsible for the prior creation of the brain. Rather than limiting his interpretation of mystical experience to a state of mysterious oneness, Newberg moves towards conventional theism in claiming that the deity is made real by "neurobiologically endorsed assurances," and that the God who stands behind these experiences "has been verified through a direct mystical encounter, as literal, absolute truth."[14]

Traditional theists question the way Newberg at times reduces the divine to the level of human consciousness, as in the following passage: "There's no other way for God to get into your head except through the brain's neural pathways. Correspondingly, God cannot exist as a concept or as reality any place else but in your mind."[15] Ilia Delio believes that Newberg's failure to make a fundamental distinction between God and other reality results in the merging of theology and science whereby God and the brain become indistinguishable.[16] In his overall critique of such an approach, Delio asks, "Is that which is experienced part of the self? transcendent to the self? personal? or wholly other? In short, what enables Newberg to name the something of the subject's personal experience during an altered state of consciousness as God—or for that matter Absolute Unitary Being—and are these, indeed, the same?" Delio refers to the deity as "the fullness of mystery that lures us into the unknown," and he describes the essence of the mystical state as beyond anything we could comprehend as finite, contingent beings.[17] Belief in the existence of God, he claims, is more than a neurological condition, and religious experience is more than a modification of neural input.

While some thinkers advance the view that since God is spirit, mystical experience transcends the arena of the sensory,[18] others claim that the interconnection of the brain and the mind means that God must be responsible for activating the appropriate areas of the brain.[19] The question then arises as to whether there could be alternative forms of brain stimulation that would produce what may be felt as a form of connection to God, even though it may not involve a mystical experience. To this end experiments have been carried out by Michael Persinger, who identifies the temporal lobe as the biological basis of what he calls "the God Experience."[20] His research involves placing an electromagnetic stimulus on the relevant part of the head. The impulses penetrate deep into the brain, where they interact with the subject's neural fields. Persinger writes, "These God experiences contain common themes of 'knowing', forced thinking, inner voices, familiarity, and sensations of uplifting movements."[21] The feelings also include a sense of deep meaning and conviction.

In Persinger's view, the brain is the cause of these experiences, which means that no information can be gained from them concerning any external reality. He proposes that a biological capacity for the God experience may originally have been necessary for the survival of the species, but that the development of our ability to master nature means there is no continuing need for the earlier experiences and beliefs. As was the case in respect of the Newberg critiques, theorists have challenged Persinger's theory on the grounds that religious truth cannot be reduced to the effects of brain stimulus, the actual presence of God being beyond anything that could ever be established by scientific testing.[22]

The manner in which the findings of altered states of consciousness are interpreted in the individual case will inevitably be influenced by the person's prior beliefs. In the Newberg experiments, the Buddhist monks reported "a sense of timelessness and infinity, feeling part of everyone and everything in existence." For the nuns on the other hand, the experience was described as "a tangible sense of the closeness of God and a mingling with Him."[23] It was suggested in Chapter 10 that when individuals hold to the idea that a vast gulf exists between finite beings and an infinite God, the oneness experienced will be interpreted in a way that preserves the separate identities of the human and the divine. With regard to the Newberg study, the neural patterns of the monks and the nuns were reported as being identical, but the interpretations of their altered states of consciousness reflected the differences in their respective belief systems. Because we generally rely on our own experience to determine the truth or falsity of positions adopted by others, we would probably evaluate the differing beliefs of the two groups on the basis of what we have previously accepted as true. The question then arises as to whether we have any method of determining which of the two interpretations is "correct." (This question will be addressed in Chapter 13.)

Altered states of consciousness can be interpreted as being nothing more than changes in brain states caused by sensory deprivation. Alternatively, they can be seen as an experience given by a personal transcendent God, whose existence cannot be established through scientific inquiry. With regard to the attempts made to prove that a personal God exists because he is experienced, those experiences, like all others, are mediated through the brain. There would be no difference, however, between the brain scan of a person who claims to be experiencing God in a situation where God actually exists, and the scan of such a person if God does not exist. The studies involving the nuns and the monks revealed no differences in brain states, even though the former group were committed to the existence of a personal God while the latter group were not.[24]

An alternative to the two forms of interpretation discussed above is based on the information presented in Chapter 8. There it was explained that in the view of some scientists, humans are multidimensional beings who are integral to the multidimensionality of the universe. On that basis, the altered brain patterns in studies such as those of Newberg would not be reducible to mere three-dimensional changes to the brain's neural pathways, nor could such changes be attributable to the activity of a divine being. The most likely explanation is that the brain patterns occurring in mystical states reflect the idea that the brain is the physical form in which higher dimensional reality is expressed.

Although the evidence produced up to this point would suggest the oneness of all reality, certain individuals within the religious traditions who hold conventional views report life-transforming experiences as a result of the beliefs they hold, and some of these reports are outlined in the next chapter. Later it will be suggested that the experience of transformation does not depend on the factual accuracy of the beliefs embraced.

1 For a detailed discussion on the sensory systems, see Wim van den Dungen, "A Neurophilosophy of Sensation," Antwerp, (2014), *www.neuro.sofiatopia.org/brainmind sensation.htm*.

2 Andrew Newberg and Mark Robert Waldman, *Why We Believe What We Believe*, (New York: Free Press, 2006), 67–68.

3 Andrew Newberg, Eugene d'Aquili, and Vince Rause, *Why God Won't Go Away: Brain Science and the Biology of Belief,*

(New York, Ballantine Books, 2002), 7.

4 Newberg and Waldman, (2006), 84.

5 Newberg et al (2002), 119.

6 Ibid., 147.

7 Ibid., 155.

8 Jonathan Scott Miller, "Are Mystical Experiences Evidence for the Existence of a Transcendent Reality? Evaluating Eugene d'Aquili and Andrew Newberg's Argument for Absolute Unitary Being," *Florida Philosophical Review*, IX, 1, (2009), 50.

9 Ibid., 47.

10 Matthew Ratcliffe, "Neurotheology: A Science of What?" in Patrick McNamara (ed.), *The Neurology of Religious Experience*, (Portsmouth, NH: Greenwood Publishing Group Inc., 2006), 99. Ratcliffe gives an example of meditation on a cat, claiming that the readouts in this case could not indicate the existence of the cat, because we lack any corresponding brain structures.

11 Gregory R. Peterson, "Mysterium Tremendum," *Zygon*, 37, 2, (2002), 241.

12 Newberg et al (2002), 155.

13 Eugene G. D'Aquili, Andrew P. Newberg, *The Mystical Mind: Probing the Biology of Religious Experience*, (Minneapolis: Fortress Press, 1999), 193.

14 Newberg et al (2002),164.

15 Ibid., 37.

16 Ilia Delio, "Brain Science and the Biology of Belief: A Theological Response," *Zygon*, 38, 3 (2003), 578.

17 Ibid., 584.

18 James H. Austin, *Zen and the Brain: Toward an Understanding of Meditation and Consciousness*, (Cambridge: MIT Press, 1998), 6.

19 Arthur Peacocke, "The Sound of Sheer Silence: How Does God Communicate with Humanity?" in Robert John Russell

(ed.) *Neuroscience and the Person: Scientific Perspectives on Divine Action,* (Notre Dame, IN: University of Notre Dame Press, 1999), 221.

20 Michael Persinger, "Experimental Simulation of the God Experience: Implications for Religious Beliefs and the Future of the Human Species," in Rhawn Joseph (ed.),*Neurotheology: Brain, Science, Spirituality, Religious Experience,* (San Jose, CA: University of California Press, 2002), 274.

21 ______________, *Neuropsychological Bases of God Beliefs,* (New York: Praeger Publishers, 1987), x.

22 A similar position is outlined in Anne L.C. Runehov, *Sacred or Neural? The Potential of Neuroscience to Explain Religious Experience*, (Göttingen: Vandenhoeck & Ruprecht, 2007), 213–215.

23 Newberg et al, (2002), 7.

24 Some theists would claim that since God exists, on the basis of their belief in him, the nuns would have had an experience that is not available to unbelievers. But since the brain patterns of the nuns and the monks were found to be identical, the difference between the two groups could not have been in their experiences, but in the respective ways they interpreted the event.

Chapter 12

Religious Experience

Non-mystical experience within the traditions

Up to this point in the discussion, religious concepts have been addressed mainly in the context of experiences recounted by mystics. The majority of believers, however, do not enter into the altered states of consciousness that characterise the mystical state. Some of these people nevertheless describe their experiences as life-transforming, and claim that through their faith, they have found meaning, purpose, and hope. The intense and intimate nature of these experiences has been claimed by believers and certain religious thinkers to demonstrate the reality of God's existence. Some critics, however, have challenged the possibility that such events could represent anything other than individual reactions to particular life circumstances. This chapter examines the arguments for and against the idea that the existence of the deity can be established through the experiences of believers.

Theists generally hold that our present existence is fundamentally deficient, and that there is something morally wrong with the human race. They sense that a higher form of existence is possible, and that our primary need is for salvation from the state in which we have placed ourselves through our sinfulness and disobedience. God as the all-powerful being, it is claimed, seeks to communicate with us today, and desires that we approach him in an attitude of repentance, obedience, and faith. Within the monotheisms, the deity is believed to have reached out to his creatures through his acts in history, and has chosen a given race, or certain people, on whom to bestow his favor, though a willingness to respond to the divine overtures is normally required. In some approaches, the individual is encouraged to take the initiative. The willingness of the divine to receive those who reach out to him is indicated in a statement attributed to Muhammad: "If one goes one step towards God, God comes two steps towards *him*."[1]

Religious experience can be examined on the basis of a felt need for God, and may include the emotional and even sensual awareness of his presence. The significance of these experiences is addressed by the twentieth-century philosopher and psychologist William James who seeks to discover whether there is a common core underlying experiences recounted in the various faith traditions. James suggests that feelings are the basis for the formation of belief. When we are faced with options that cannot be decided through the exercise of reason, we are justified in believing that to which our deepest or "passional" self is drawn.[2] As is the case with sensory experience, our feelings do not always correspond to reality and we sometimes consider them to be inappropriate, but the fact that we can form such conclusions indicates that emotions generally give us reliable information about the world. James' position is that all systems of thought are hypotheses to which both our emotional and logical faculties are directed, and that feelings "may be as prophetic and anticipatory of truth as anything else we have."[3]

Each of the traditions gives a prominent place to the role of the emotions in religious experience. Within Hasidic Judaism, Israel Baal Shem Tov discusses the kind of relationship with God that can arise through prayer and the study of the Torah.[4] Shem Tov was originally moved by the experiences of "simple laborers" who lacked formal knowledge, but were able to express their love for God in a most profound way.[5] The Talmud, a central text of Rabbinic Judaism, teaches that God seeks the heart, and the contemporary Jewish scholar Ismar Schorsch describes as "sensual" the experiences of God's presence, his nearness and compassion.[6] The Hasidic Rabbi Menachem M. Schneerson suggests that our emotions reflect who we are and what motivates us, and that even the strongest of our emotional resources is needed by the mind in developing qualities of character in the service of God.[7] Religious experience for the Jewish philosopher Martin Buber is characterised by a relationship between the self and the divine that he describes as "I-Thou,"[8] where God is portrayed as a caring "Thou," rather than an object-like "it."

In the context of Islamic teaching, Yasser Ad-Dab'bagh explains that the mind has two components: one is reason or intellect, and the other is "heart" (distinguished from the physical organ), which is the place where knowledge is invested with emotion, and thereby becomes conviction.[9] For Muhammad Iqbal, faith is not simply a passive belief in certain propositions, but "a living assurance begotten of rare experience,"[10] where the world comes to signify the presence, care and love of God, and where the believer has a personal and direct experience of divine grace. The nature of religious experience for the Muslim has been described as a closeness to God, and a connection to the world and to universal energies. This kind of bond promotes an enjoyment of life and stimulates within the believer "healthy awareness, sensitivity, serenity and foresight."[11] The relationship with the Creator is claimed to give light to the heart and contentment to the soul; it quietens fear and anxiety.

A different approach is taken by the Islamic thinker Adnan Aslan who challenges what he regards as the Western concept of religious experience. He points out that this description was originally used in an attempt to free Christian concepts from metaphysical beliefs and the dominance of ecclesiastical institutions, but that it is not applicable in respect of Islam. For Aslan, the transmission process and contents of the prophetic revelation are "extraordinary and miraculous," which means they cannot come within the ambit of personal religious experience.[12]

Aslan holds that since God is "infinite, transcendent, eternal, all-powerful and all-knowing," he could not be experienced by finite and mortal human beings. On the other hand, the position taken by the Islamic thinkers discussed above is supported by studies such as that carried out in Kuwait, where the questions asked of college students included whether they had "changed profoundly as a result of a religious experience." Forty-eight percent of men and fifty-two percent of women answered this question in the affirmative.[13] Religious belief in general has been shown to alleviate the fear of death and to help in overcoming addictions and life-negating behaviors. It can promote psychological growth, and lead to feelings of safety and peace by providing "comfort and hope, courage, guidance, and moral strength."[14]

The kind of experience believers may have can extend to an immediate, sensual awareness of the divine. Accounts cited by James include the following: "God is more real to me than any thought or thing or person"; "God surrounds me like the physical atmosphere. He is closer to me than my own breath."[15] These feelings are as convincing for the person as direct sensory experience. James makes an even stronger claim in suggesting that humans can feel an "objective presence," a perception of "something there"[16] that is deeper than the reliance we place on the senses. For Richard Swinburne, the recognition of God as an all-powerful and all-knowing being can result from "hearing His voice, or feeling His presence, or seeing His handiwork or by some sixth sense."[17] Similarly, Alvin Plantinga writes that beliefs such as "God disapproves of what I have done," and "God forgives me" are as basic to experience as a whole as is the perception of an object.[18] The inclusion in the sacred texts of narratives where God revealed himself to certain individuals by means of the senses has led researchers to investigate the extent to which people of today claim to have experienced God through forms of sensory perception. In 2004 a large number of American students from a state university and a Christian college were asked about their view of God in regard to the five basic sensory modalities. The findings included a depiction of God as being "closer, smoother, softer, and warmer" rather than "far away, rougher, harder, and colder."[19]

A further area examined by researchers concerns an aspect of religious experience referred to in a Christian context as "conversion," where a wholehearted commitment to the faith replaces a nominal adherence or an absence of interest in religious questions. In a study involving Harvard/Radcliffe students, many of them reported that through their conversion experience they had found a new meaning and purpose in life. The majority felt they had "more spiritual resources, more tolerance and concern for others, less self-hatred, fewer feelings of hopelessness and despair, and less fear of death."[20] Some of them changed their career goals towards the helping professions, and nearly all stopped using drugs and alcohol. Another study involved 130 students at a Midwestern university in the United States. Those who claimed to have had a conversion experience reported "positive life transformation and significant improvements in their sense of self."[21] Overall, the experience of conversion has been described as "a radical reorganization of one's identity, meaning, and purpose in life."[22] Both the emotional content of experiences reported by believers, together with the profound changes consequential to such events, have helped to confirm the belief held in a reality that is beyond the limitations of everyday existence.

Insights from psychology

Various mainstream theories in the field of psychology have been applied in examining the nature of non-mystical religious experience. One of these theories concerns the kind of bond an infant develops with her primary care giver.[23] John Bowlby proposes that a natural process has evolved whereby infants manifest a strong need to maintain proximity with their care giver in order to be protected from external dangers. This attachment system is activated when the infant is alarmed, causing her to engage in behaviors that seek to re-establish proximity.[24] Subsequent research has shown that developments in personality will generally reflect patterns established at the beginning of life.[25] Infants who feel secure in being able to trust the reliability and responsiveness of the care giver are likely to have a healthy level of trust in others, while those who experience continual neglect will tend to avoid closeness in their relationships. An inconsistent response from the care giver will cause the infant to become anxious and to have ambivalent feelings towards others.

Attachment models have been linked to religious experience, and are based on the view that God can have the function of an attachment figure.[26] Research has shown that believers with positive experiences in infancy seek to maintain a sense of proximity to God; they regard him as a haven of safety and a secure base, and they trust his response in times of adversity.[27] In an American study conducted in 1997, participants who felt secure in early life perceived God as being more loving than those who had undergone negative experiences. Participants who had been neglected were most likely to be agnostic, while many of those who had developed anxiety reported a religiously transforming experience.[28] For the latter group, belief in God was interpreted as compensating for the earlier insecure attachment relationship. Similar findings occur in research conducted within Islamic societies.[29] Among Jewish believers, a study in 2004 found that subjects who had experienced optimal attachment in infancy were more likely to view God as loving, approving, and caring.[30] The profound effect of early experiences indicates the likelihood that individuals will develop the idea of a deity who has the qualities that were instrumental in helping to form their basic personalities. This psychological reality could not therefore, of itself, be used in an argument for the existence of God.

The evidential value of religious experience

In response to the claim that religious events are not simply a product of concepts and beliefs about the deity,[31] and that there can be a direct awareness of God that is as convincing to the individual as the various modes of sense perception,[32] it has been argued that if an experience of God could provide evidence that he actually exists, there must be ways of separating genuine from delusive experiences, and also of establishing what condition a person would have to be in so as to have the experience. Since neither of these requirements can be met, the existence of the purported object of the experience cannot be verified. There would be no way, therefore, to confirm or disconfirm the truth claimed for the experience.[33] Furthermore, since there are wide variations in the kinds of experiences described by believers, the idea that God is encountered in these experiences may represent nothing more than an interpretation of what is occurring. Similarly, in a situation where God is believed to have certain characteristics, a person may simply develop an emotional response to the qualities envisaged. An additional argument advanced is that in order to know without a doubt that it was God who was being encountered, it would be necessary for the individual to perceive a being who was all-knowing, all-powerful, and all-good. Such attributes, however, could never form part of a perception.[34]

With regard to psychological explanations for religious claims, theists have asserted that even if professionals in the field are able to explain the reason for a particular belief, that in itself could not establish that the belief in question is false.[35] What has to be determined is whether or not the reasons for engagement with the belief are rational, since a strong desire could lead a person to believe in something for which the evidence is lacking. Defenders of theism also point out that although a psychologist may uncover factors that could prejudice a person towards adopting a particular religious belief, it would be impossible for anyone to demonstrate that such a prejudice was the determining cause of the belief.[36]

The claim by James that feeling is the basic factor in religious experience is questioned by Wayne Proudfoot, who argues that writers such as James are seeking to protect religion from scrutiny by locating religious faith in a personal, private realm, and that religious feelings and beliefs should be investigated in the same way as other cultural phenomena. According to Proudfoot, the reason for a given experience being described as religious, thereby indicating the existence of God, is that the individual would regard this description as the most likely explanation.[37] In claiming that belief is the primary or formative element in religious experiences, Proudfoot is dismissing the possibility that the experiences themselves could be a validating factor in religious belief. William Barnard asserts that Proudfoot's ideas reduce religion to a "cultural, public, accessible phenomenon."[38] Although the profound inner sense described by James cannot be explained merely by an individual's acceptance of the basic tenets of her faith, this does not imply that the experience is thereby quarantined from the relevant beliefs, as Proudfoot's critique of James would suggest. Religious experience occurs in the context of a person's trust in a divine being, and includes the belief that such a being is the cause of the experience.

Arguments for the existence of God based on religious experience are inadequate to establish conclusively that a personal God exists. On the other hand, many people have experiences that are sufficiently powerful for them either to become believers, or to have their faith in God confirmed. From the evidence available, it is difficult to deny that something out of the ordinary is happening in the lives of these people, both in terms of the intensity of their experiences, and in the processes of transformation that result. What that mysterious element may be is examined in the next chapter, where it will be suggested that experiences interpreted as religious arise from complex operations within the psyche, and that truth for a given individual cannot be determined on the basis of external factors, but is constituted of that which gives meaning to a person's existence.

1 Śesharāva More, *Islam, maker of the Muslim mind,* (Pune, India: Rajhans Prakashan, 2004), 567.
2 William James, *The Will to Believe and Other Essays in Popular Philosophy,* (New York: Cosimo, Inc., 2007), 11.
3 __________, *Essays in Radical Empiricism,* (New York: Cosimo Inc., 2008), 130.
4 The Torah consists of the first five books of the Hebrew scriptures. Shem Tov was also interested in mystical experience (see Chapter 10).
5 "A Knowing Heart" in *Sichos In Which The Rebbe Advanced Our Emotional Frontiers, from The Works of The Lubavitcher Rebbe, Rabbi Menachem M. Schneerson,* Rabbi Eliyahu Touger, (trans.) (New York: Sichos In English, 2002).
6 Ismar Schorsch, "The Sacred Cluster: The Core Values of Conservative Judaism," (1995), www.jewishvirtuallibrary.org/.../Judaism/conservative_values.html.Cached—SimilarYou + 1'd this publicly. Undo.
7 "A Knowing Heart" (2002).
8 For an exposition of Buber's work, see Kenneth Paul Kramer, *Martin Buber's I and Thou: practising living dialogue,* (Mahwah, NU: Paulist Press, 2003).
9 Yasser Ad-Dab'bagh, "The Transformative Effect of Seeking the Eternal: A Sampling of the Perspectives of Two Great Muslim Intellectuals-Ibn-Hazm and Al-Ghazali," *Psychoanalytic Inquiry*, 28, 5 (2008), 552.
10 Muhammad Iqbal, "The Reconstruction of Religious

Thought in Islam", ed. M. Saeed Sheikh, (Lahore: Institute of Islamic Culture, 1996), cited in Mohammad Iqbal Afaqi, "Knowledge, Belief and Faith: A Comparative Study of Christian and Islamic Epistemologies," PhD dissertation submitted to The University of the Punjab, Lahore, (2003), 7.

11 Syed Qutb, Commentary on Surah 103 – The Declining Day a'Asr, *web.youngmuslims.ca/online_library/tafsir/syed_qutb/surah_103.htm*.

12 Adnan Aslan, "What is Wrong with the Concept of Religious Experience?", *Islam and Christian-Muslim Relations*, 14, 3, (2003), 305.

13 Alessandra L. Gonzáles, "Measuring Religiosity in a Majority Muslim Context: Gender, Religious Salience and Religious Experience Among Kuwaiti College Students – A Research Note," *Journal for the Scientific Study of Religion*, 50, 2, (2011), 345.

14 Caroline Franks Davis, *The Evidential Force of Religious Experience*, (Oxford: Clarendon Press, 1989), 247.

15 William James, *The Varieties of Religious Experience: A Study In Human Nature*, (Rockville, MD: Arc Manor, 2008), 59.

16 Ibid., 49.

17 Richard Swinburne, *The Existence of God*, (Oxford, Clarendon Press, 1979), 268.

18 Alvin Plantinga, "Is Belief in God Properly Basic? *Noûs*, 15, 1, (1981), 46.

19 Paul Chara and Jill N. Gillett, "Sensory Images of God: Divine Synesthesia?" *Journal of Psychology and Christianity*, 23, 3, (2004), 234–248. The various findings were interpreted as examples of synesthesia, where the simulation of one sense modality elicits a perception in a different sense modality.

20 Armand M. Nicholi, "A new dimension of youth culture," *American Journal of Psychiatry*, 131 (1974), 396–401.

21 Brian J. Zinnbauer and Kenneth I. Pargament, "Spiritual Conversion: A Study of Religious Change Among College Students," *Journal for the Scientific Study of Religion*, 37, 1, (1998), 165.

22 Arthur J. Schwartz, "The Nature of Spiritual Transformation: A Review of the Literature," (2000), *www.spiritualtransformationresearch.org*, 5, www.metanexus.net/archive/.../pdf/STSRP-LiteratureReview2–7.PDF.

23 Another attempt to relate religious belief and experience to psychological states is that of Sigmund Freud, who suggests that the child sees the father both as the powerful protector and as the punitive authority figure. These feelings are transferred to God, who becomes a father substitute. See Christopher N. Chapman, *Freud, Religion, and Anxiety*, (Morrisville NC: Lulu.com, 2007), 33.

24 John Bowlby, *Attachment and Loss*, Vol. 1, Attachment, (New York: Basic Books, 1982).

25 Lee A. Kirkpatrick and Phillip R. Shaver, "Attachment Theory and Religion: Childhood Attachments, Religious Experience, and Conversion," *Journal for the Scientific Study of Religion*, 29, 3, (1990), 329.

26 _______________, "The role of attachment in religious belief and behavior," in Daniel Perlman and Kim Bartholomew (eds.), *Advances in Personal Relationships*, vol. 5, 239–65, (London: Jessica Kingsley, 1994); Lee A. Kirkpatrick, *Attachment, evolution, and the psychology of religion*, (New York: Guilford Press, 2005).

27 Anupam Kumari and R. S. Pirta, "Exploring Human Relationship with God as a Secure Base," *Journal of the Indian Academy of Applied Psychology*, 35, (October 2009), 119.

28 Lee A. Kirkpatrick, "A Longitudinal Study of Changes in Religious Belief and Behavior as a Function of Individual Differences in Adult Attachment Style," *Journal for the*

Scientific Study of Religion, 36, 2, (1997), 213.

29 Fawzyiah Hadi and Ghenaim Al-Fayez, "Islamic Arabic Youth and Family Development" in Richard M. Lerner (ed.), *Handbook of Applied Developmental Science*, Vol. 3, (Thousand Oaks, CA: Sage Publications Inc., 2003), 470.

30 Mario Mikulincer and Phillip R. Shaver, *Attachment in Adulthood*, (New York: Guilford Publications, Inc., 2007), 247.

31 Keith E. Yandell, *The Epistemology of Religious Experience*, (Cambridge: Cambridge University Press, 1993), 216.

32 William P. Alston, *Perceiving God: The Epistemology of Religious Experience*, (New York: Cornell University Press, 1991), 36.

33 Nick Trakakis (ed.), *William L. Rowe on Philosophy of Religion: Selected Writings*, (Aldershot, Hampshire: Ashgate Publishing Limited, 2007), 380.

34 Nick Zangwill, "The myth of religious experience," *Religious Studies*, 40, (2004), 1.

35 Alfred C. Ewing, "Awareness of God," *Philosophy*, 40, 151 (1965), 6.

36 Ibid.

37 Wayne Proudfoot, *Religious Experience*, (Berkeley: University of California Press, 1985), 108.

38 G. William Barnard, "Explaining the Unexplainable: Wayne Proudfoot's 'Religious Experience,'" *Journal of the American Academy of Religion*, Vol. 60, No. 2 (Summer, 1992), 232.

Chapter 13

Transcendence

In recent times, Western societies have witnessed a plethora of books written by individuals who have had life-changing experiences.[1] According to the authors, similar experiences are available to anyone who is willing to accept the ideas they outline, and to take the steps they prescribe. Although they may have little interest in the idea of a personal, transcendent God, the zeal with which these authors advocate their own particular beliefs and methods, parallels the approach of theists who claim that their deity is the one true God, and that only he can meet an individual's deepest needs. Members of both groups seem to assume that other systems of belief and behavior are either wrong or are lacking in certain essential elements. One of the aims of this book has been to challenge the exclusivity of such assumptions.[2]

For most of human history, there has been a need to attribute causes to particular events, and to find answers to life's mysteries. Questions raised have included "Why were we born only eventually to die? What happens to us after death? What is our place in the universe? Why is there suffering? What sustains and animates the universe? How was the universe made, and how long will the universe last? How can we live in this world and not be afraid?"[3] Earlier cultures postulated the idea of invisible, powerful beings who ruled the forces of nature. Described as "gods," these beings were believed to take an interest in the behavior of earthly creatures, sometimes requiring them to make sacrifices in order to secure the well-being of the group. John Hick writes: "Men seem always to have had some dim sense of the divine, expressed in the religious practices of which there is evidence extending back half a million years or more."[4]

With the advent of the modern era in about the sixteenth century, it was believed that scientific discoveries would give us access to all forms of knowledge. A consequence was the marginalization of religious faith and experience. Within mainstream thought, there were two approaches to our understanding of the world: one held that the only reality we can know is that which is produced in our minds; the other claimed that the senses provide us with direct awareness of the things in our environment.[5]

Among the attempts made to reconcile these two approaches, Edward Caird proposed the existence of a unity underlying all apparent oppositions. In place of the differences held to exist between the mental and the physical, or the subjective and the objective, Caird suggested that the two should be regarded merely as distinctions within the ultimate unity.[6] Referring to this reality as the Absolute, Caird argues that through a process of development, this mysterious concept grows in its own self-recognition in its interaction with finite beings.[7] Caird's view is that there is no separation between ourselves and the Absolute, since we are each a unique expression of that mysterious reality.

If it is true that we all participate in the Absolute, a commonality in our thinking would be expected that goes beyond the differences in our individual views. Joseph Campbell writes of a human connection to universal truth expressed in myths that have common themes across cultures.[8] Among these are stories of expulsion from paradise, floods that cover the earth, virgin births, and heroes who die and are resurrected. Myth enables us to connect with universal meaning; its power lies beneath the individual facts of particular myths. Whether or not the stories are literally true is of no relevance to the psychological and spiritual truths they express. Myth reconciles the apparent contradiction between our individual existence and that which lies beyond us. In Campbell's view, myths address our basic existential dilemma "that in the beginning we were united with the source, but that we were separated from it and now we must find a way to return."[9]

Various writers holding religious beliefs claim that people who are presented with evidence of God's existence, either by argument or through the experience of others, and who still refuse to believe in him are "psychologically or cognitively deficient."[10] William James describes an "inaptitude for religious faith" that derives from certain beliefs about the world that inhibit the natural tendency of religious faculties to expand.[11] A further explanation given by James is that individuals can have lower "susceptibilities of emotional excitement" and "affective response capacity," and that in a religious sense, these people could be regarded as "anaesthetic."

In an approach similar to that of James, religious sensitivity has been likened to a responsiveness to music.[12] The sociologist Max Weber writes: "It is true that I am absolutely unmusical religiously and have no need or ability to erect any psychic edifices of a religious character within me. But a thorough self-examination has told me that I am neither antireligious nor irreligious."[13] Since he applied Christian principles in his research, Weber apparently did not see any inconsistency in his adoption of these ideas and the fact that he lacked any religious feeling. The situation for Weber is in some ways similar to that of individuals who make a rational decision to embrace a particular faith, but whose changed or modified behavior may not be associated with any profound life-changing experience.[14] If total reliance is placed on the belief that God exists, and on the adoption of prescribed practices, rituals and behavior, the personal changes that result may be confined to the area of those beliefs and behaviors. In the Christian scriptures, the efforts that could be made by a person are given only minimal recognition. The apostle Paul describes the futility of attempts by individuals to rely on their own endeavors, or to trust in their own strength.

His teaching is that it is only through the indwelling power of the Holy Spirit (a member of the Godhead) that any genuine transformation can take place. Within himself, Paul writes, there is "nothing good,"[15] and he describes his religious experience in terms of "Not I, but Christ in me."[16] Among the evidence of a relationship with God that Paul discusses is a list of qualities described as "fruit of the Spirit."[17] These relate mainly to inner states rather than to specific behaviors or observances.

Sincere believers who for whatever reason are unable to enter into intense religious experiences will normally receive support from their leaders, whose primary concern is that people exercise faith by adopting the "correct" doctrines about God as outlined in the sacred texts. Faith is of paramount importance in each of the traditions. The Hebrew scriptures describe Abraham as being commended and subsequently blessed by God because of his faith.[18] Similarly the Koran states, "Righteousness comes from a secure faith, from sincere devotion to Allah, and from unselfish service to humankind."[19] Christian teaching is that "without faith it is impossible to please God."[20] This statement seems to indicate an obligation to exercise faith. On the other hand, faith is described as "the gift of God,"[21] which would suggest that unless God chooses to grant this gift to a given individual, there would be no hope for such a person. In a Christian context, it has sometimes been said that the following three aspects of the religious life are in descending order of importance: fact, faith, feeling.[22] The adoption of such an approach means that when the first two elements are in place, the last is reduced almost to the status of an optional extra. For believers who are firmly established in their tradition, and have exercised the required faith in God and in the essential doctrines, the question of whether or not their inner state of being has been profoundly affected may remain unaddressed.

It is not only the monotheisms that claim to have answers to the human condition.[23] Apart from the writers of self-help books, alternatives are provided by members of the helping professions that are concerned with the problems of everyday living. In these disciplines, a commonly-held belief is that individuals have within themselves the ability to meet their need for wholeness or integration. Attention is often given to those deep areas of consciousness that are not immediately accessible to the person, but are believed to exert a powerful influence on feelings and behavior.

Most forms of therapy hold that what we believe at a conscious level may have little relationship to our beliefs at a much deeper level. For example, a woman who is outstandingly successful in her career and in her role as a wife and mother, may have endured overwhelming pain in her formative years. Although she may consciously believe that she is a worthwhile person, at a much deeper level of consciousness she may see herself as worthless. In the safety of the therapeutic setting, memories of earlier painful experiences can be uncovered, and if through this process, the woman comes to recognise her intrinsic worth, her life may be transformed.

A further context in which transformation can occur is through the reading of books by contemporary writers who have had life-changing experiences. With regard to the various ways we have of achieving a sense of wholeness, James points out that "to find religion is only one out of many ways of reaching unity ... the process of remedying inner incompleteness and reducing inner discord is a general psychological process, which may take place with any sort of mental material, and need not necessarily assume the religious form."[24]

James' view of the variety of ways that human fulfillment can be experienced is generally not shared by the religious traditions, each of which claims to have "the truth." This situation is paralleled in the areas of therapy and self-help. Among the earlier psychological analysts, conflicting views were advanced regarding the effects of sexual repression, the need to integrate the diverse elements of the psyche, or the striving for power. Later approaches addressed the effects of conditioning, and the unrecognised beliefs that control our behavior. In the modern self-help movement, authors discuss their own unique methods of finding peace after periods of despair.

Because of the wide variations among systems of thought that offer the hope of personal transformation, no single set of ideas could have a valid claim to be effective for everyone. Whether or not a particular set of beliefs has the potential to be life transforming for a given person will be determined by the relationship between the ideas themselves and the personality structure of the individual, together with the cumulative effects of changing circumstances and influences in the person's life. For example, someone who at a deep level of consciousness sees herself as evil, may respond to the message that universal moral failing is of such a magnitude that only the death of God's son could atone for the sins of the entire human race.

The motivation for a person's desire to embrace a religious faith could be a sense that her life is incomplete. This situation is discussed by Ilia Delio, who asks, "Why are human beings in their biological composition not self-sufficient, self-contained, and completely fulfilled entities? .... What impels us to seek relationship with an other outside and beyond ourselves?"[25] For a person with a Christian faith, these questions could be answered in terms of the statement addressed to God by Bishop Augustine in the fourth century: "[T]hou hast made us for thyself and restless is our heart until it comes to rest in thee."[26] Similar thoughts are expressed in the texts of Judaism[27] and Islam.[28] Those who have had the experience of religious conversion may contrast their previous feeling of a divided sense of self with their new sense of a complete and transformed self.[29] The yearning we have to connect with something that seems to be beyond or greater than ourselves, is described by Gillian Ross as "the primary aspiration of the human condition."[30] Similarly,

Václav Havel writes of the need for transcendence—a state he describes as one of being in harmony with "what we do not understand, what seems distant from us in time and space, but with which we are nevertheless mysteriously linked."[31]

In a previous chapter we looked at the idea outlined in string theory that the universe is in ten spatial dimensions.[32] It was also proposed that we are multidimensional beings. This claim has direct relevance to the question of beliefs and personal transformation. If our complete existence, including our consciousness, were nothing more than three-dimensional materiality, it would seem unlikely that we could experience a sense of connectedness to something greater than ourselves, or that we would even have a longing for that ultimate state of being.

Earlier it was suggested that the experience of union can be obtained through altered states of consciousness. The paths leading to these mystical states will vary in accordance with the life circumstances and capacities of the individual. In seeking to understand their experiences, people with religious beliefs may choose to retain the idea that a gulf separates the human and the divine. Others with different beliefs may attempt to describe their feelings of oneness, only to acknowledge that their words are "hopelessly inadequate to convey the immensity and shattering impact" of what they have experienced.[33]

Theorists in various fields have taken an interest in these experiences, and some of them have presented the view that our minds are individual expressions of the universal mind.[34] Karen Armstrong replaces the traditional view of God as "a separate, external reality and judge" with the idea that the divine is "somehow one with the ground of each person's being."[35] Within Sufism, the universe is seen as a "global being," whose faculties find expression in human beings and in every other aspect of reality. Ibn Arabi writes that "the universe discovers itself through our discovery of it as ourselves."[36] A similar idea is expressed by Stanislav Grof: "When we reach experiential identification with Absolute Consciousness, we realize that our own being is ultimately commensurate with the entire cosmic network, with all of existence. The recognition of our own divine nature, our identity with the cosmic source, is the most important discovery we can make during the process of deep self-exploration."[37]

A person whose life has been transformed by her religious beliefs may wish to share her faith with others. Within the monotheisms, the basis of such an approach would be that the ideas presented constitute historical fact concerning the one true God and what he requires of us. It is here that the definition of "fact" can become a problem. Because we see ourselves as embodied creatures in a three-dimensional world, and because of the amazing discoveries made by scientists about the way that world functions, we have good reason to believe that any idea must be either right or wrong. For example, an incorrect calculation made by a structural engineer could result in a disaster. If it were the case that everything in the universe, including ourselves, were contained within three dimensions, whatever we happened to believe could be regarded as fact or as potential fact, and if shown to be true, would have universal applicability. In the context of religious faith, however, the acceptance of this limited approach to the question of truth would help to explain the extreme measures taken by certain groups throughout history and up to the present day that have sought to impose their particular beliefs on whole societies.

In the Introduction to this book, reference was made to the fact that contrasting ideas from the different faith traditions can result in similar kinds of transformation in the lives of the individuals who embrace them. The words "truth" and "untruth" were tentatively used with reference to these differing doctrinal positions. It can now be seen that when it comes to the question of who we are and what we can become, the critical factor is the way a particular set of ideas translates within our individual personality structure. In this situation, the question of right and wrong becomes irrelevant.

It may happen that a person who is raised in a family or culture that has a strong religious tradition, will initially accept the beliefs of that faith. But should it turn out that at the level of experience, the ideas do not resonate deeply within the person, she may decide to have nothing to do with religion at all. Alternatively, she may decide to investigate other traditions.[38] In recent years, many people raised in nominally Christian cultures have converted to Islam. It is estimated that in the United States, up to 25,000 people per year become Muslims. In research carried out on the reasons for these changes, the primary reported factors were "the appeal of Muslim moral values and dissatisfaction with one's former faith."[39] Cases have similarly been recorded where people from an Islamic tradition have converted to Christianity[40] or to Judaism.[41]

Individuals who firmly believe that the tenets of their faith are accurate and are binding on all humanity, may overlook the fact that for a person's life to be transformed, it is not simply a question of commitment to a particular set of beliefs. Although some changes in behavior may occur at an outward level, genuine transformation occurs at a more profound level—one to which the person may not have direct access. Where a culture is saturated in a religious tradition, those for whom such beliefs have little effect may simply conform to the various requirements without thinking about the deeper implications of what they believe. On the other hand, a devout person who accepts everything she has been taught about God and what he requires of us, but who lacks any sense of inner change, may experience feelings of failure when she sees evidence of transformation in the lives of others. It could be the case that for such a person, a different set of ideas would have the desired effect. Among these would be the concepts underlying an alternative faith tradition, a particular form of therapy, or the work of a writer in the self-help movement. The fact that individuals can experience life transformation through engaging with any of these systems of thought, demonstrates that none of them can claim universal validity.

Among modern thinkers in the West, a view has arisen that there are no objective facts, and that we each "construct" a reality based on our individual perceptions of what is true. From one perspective, the ideas advocated in this book would seem to be in accord with such a view, since contrasting beliefs have been presented as being equally life transforming for the individuals who embrace them. The basic difference between these two ways of looking at human perceptions is that the concept of a universe in ten spatial dimensions may eventually be established as a fact, having equal validity with the idea that the earth rotates on its axis and revolves around the sun. If the former theory comes to be scientifically accepted, at the ultimate level of the dimensions there may be a confluence of objective and subjective truth, the objectivity of the conscious universe finding expression in the subjectivity of the individual.

Challenges to the idea of a personal God are considerable, whether originating in philosophy or in science, but in the end, it is transformation that is the question of fundamental human concern. Factual knowledge that sustains us at the level of our three-dimensional existence proves inadequate when it comes to finding personal fulfillment. The deep-seated need we have to reach that goal and to experience a state of transcendence can lead us in many directions. Some of these will include the idea that a personal God loves us and wants to be in a relationship with us. Should an engagement with the divine fulfill our deepest needs, we may assume that a form of interconnectedness is occurring at the deepest level of our being. This may be the case even when we hold the view that a vast gulf exists between ourselves and the Creator. Alternatively, we may come to accept that the apparent conflict between an identity with the transcendent, and the idea that we are individuals, separate from all other reality, can be resolved through the awareness that each of us is a unique expression of that ultimate mystery.

1 Examples would include the works of Louise L. Hay, her earliest book being *You Can Heal Your Life*, (Carlsbad, CA: Hay House, 1984).
2 See Chapter 7 for the differences in philosophical positions regarding the question of God, and the impossibility of determining which is the "correct" view.
3 Andrew Newberg et al (2002), 61.
4 John Hick, *God Has Many Names*, (Louisville: Westminster John Knox Press, 2000), 43.
5 See Chapter 1.
6 Edward Caird, "Metaphysic," *Essays on Literature and Philosophy*, Vol. 2, (Glasgow: MacLehose, 1892), 442.
7 William Mander, "Edward Caird and British Idealist Philosophy," address given at Oxford University, 20 January 1998.
8 Joseph Campbell, *Myths to Live By* (New York: Viking Press, 1972).
9 Cited in Andrew Newberg et al (2002), 91.
10 Jennifer Faust, "Can religious arguments persuade?", *International Journal for Philosophy of Religion*, 63, (2008), 71.
11 William James, *The Varieties of Religious Experience*, (New York: Longmans, Green, and Co., 1902), 204. For a commentary on the lasting influence of James' thought, see Theo Anderson, "One Hundred Years of 'Pragmatism,'" *The Wilson Quarterly*, 31, 3 (Summer, 2007).
12 On the differences between individuals regarding a capacity to experience the spiritual, Richard Rorty writes, "One can be tone deaf when it comes to religion, just as one can be oblivious to the charms of music. People who find

themselves quite unable to take an interest in the question of whether God exists have no right to be contemptuous of people who believe passionately in his existence or of people who deny it with equal passion. Nor do either of the latter have a right to be contemptuous of those to whom the dispute seems pointless." R. Rorty, "Anti-clericalism and atheism," in Mark A. Wrathall (ed.), *Religion After Metaphysics*, (Cambridge: Cambridge University Press, 2003), 38.

13 Marianne Weber, *Max Weber: A biography*, (New Brunswick, N.J.: Transaction, 1988), 324, cited in William H. Swatos, Jr. and Peter Kivisto, "Max Weber as 'Christian Sociologist,'" *Journal for the Scientific Study of Religion*, 30, 4 (1991), 347.

14 See Chapter 11 for examples of powerful religious feeling reported by adherents of the various traditions.

15 Romans 7: 18.

16 Galatians 2: 20.

17 Galatians 5: 22–23.

18 Genesis 15:6.

19 Note 28 to Quran 2:4.

20 Hebrews 11: 6.

21 Ephesians 2: 8.

22 An exposition of this position is given in William Evans, *The Great Doctrines of the Bible*, (Glendale, CA: Bibliotech Press, 2014), 114.

23 The focus of the book has been the question of God, due to the significance this question has for millions of people throughout the world. In this final chapter, the scope is being widened to include the possibility of other forms of life transformation, since in modern Western culture people are turning away from traditional religious beliefs and are embracing alternative ways of being.

24 James, *The Varieties of Religious Experience*, 175.

25 Ilia Delio, "Brain Science and the Biology of Belief: A

Theological Response," *Zygon*, 38, 3 (2003): 580.

26 *Saint Augustine:* Confessions and Enchiridion, (ed. and trans.) Albert C. Outler (Louisville, KY: Westminster John Knox Press, 1955), 25.

27 Psalm 42.

28 Quran 31:3 and 69:4.

29 See Brian J. Zinnbauer and Kenneth I. Pargament, "Spiritual Conversion: A Study of Religious Change Among College Students," *Journal for the Scientific Study of Religion*, 37, no. 1, (1998).

30 Gillian Ross, *Psyche's Yearning: Radical Perspectives on Self Transformation* (Bloomington, IN: Trafford Publishing, 2010), 22.

31 Václav Havel, "A sense of the transcendent," in *The Art of the Impossible: Politics as Morality in Practice*, (New York: Knopf, 1997).

32 See Chapter 8.

33 Stanislav Grof, *The Cosmic Game: Explorations in the Frontiers of Human Consciousness*, (New York: State University of New York Press, 1998), 27.

34 Paul Davies, *God and the New Physics*, (London: Penguin Books Ltd., 1983), 210.

35 Karen Armstrong, *A History of God*, (New York: Ballantine Books, 1993), 269.

36 Pir Vilayat Inayat Khan, "Toward a Unified Worldview: New Perspectives in Science & Spirituality," www.embracingthecontradiction.org/unified.htm.

37 Grof, op. cit., 38.

38 These alternative systems of thought may include those of the Eastern traditions.

39 Audrey A. Maslim and Jeffrey P. Bjorck, "Reasons for Conversion to Islam Among Women in the United States," *Psychology of Religion and Spirituality*, Vol. 1, 2, (2009): 97.

40 Viggo Mortensen, (ed.,) *Theology and the Religions: A*

Dialogue, (Michigan: Wm. B. Eerdmans Publishing Co., 2003), 301.

41 David Novak, Randi Rashkover, *Tradition in the Public Square: A David Novak Reader*, (Norwich: SCM Press, 2008), 240.

References

Academy of Sciences of Berlin, Editors. *Gottfried Wilhelm Leibniz: Sämtliche Schriften und Briefe*, VI, 1923.

Adam, James, Editor. *The Republic of Plato*. Cambridge: Cambridge University Press, 2009.

Ad-Dab'bagh, Yasser. "The Transformative Effect of Seeking the Eternal: A Sampling of the Perspectives of Two Great Muslim Intellectuals-Ibn-Hazm and Al-Ghazali." *Psychoanalytic Inquiry*, 28, 5, 2008.

Alston, William P. *Perceiving God: The Epistemology of Religious Experience*. New York: Cornell University Press, 1991.

Anderson, Theo. "One Hundred Years of 'Pragmatism.'" *The Wilson Quarterly*, 31, 3, 2007.

Anselm, *Proslogion*. Translated by Thomas Williams. Indianapolis: Hackett Publishing Company Inc., 2001.

Appleby, Peter C. "Mysticism and Ineffability." *International Journal for Philosophy of Religion*, 11, no. 3, 1980.

Aristotle *Physics: Book VIII*. Translated by Daniel W. Graham. Oxford: Oxford University Press, 1999.

Armstrong, Karen. *A History of God*. London: Vintage, 1999.

________ *Islam: A Short History*. New York: The Modern Library, 2002.

Ash, David. *Vortex of Energy: A Scientific Theory*. Berkshire, UK: Puja Power Publications, 2012.

Aslan, Adnan. "What Is Wrong with the Concept of Religious Experience?". *Islam and Christian-Muslim Relations*, 14, no. 3, 2003.

Austin, James H. *Zen and the Brain: Toward an Understanding of Meditation and Consciousness*, Cambridge: MIT Press, 1998.

Bailey, Steven. "Can Spirituality Be Taught?", *www.lookstein.org/online_journal.php?id=125*.

Barnard, G. William. "Explaining the Unexplainable: Wayne

Proudfoot's 'Religious Experience.'" *Journal of the American Academy of Religion*, 60, no. 2, 1992.

Bello, Angela Ales. *The Divine in Husserl and Other Explorations*. Analecta Husserliana, Vol. XCVIII, Dordrecht: Springer, 2009.

Bennington, Geoffrey and Jacques Derrida. *Jacques Derrida*. Translated by Geoffrey Bennington. Chicago: University of Chicago Press, 1993.

Benson, Bruce Ellis. *Pious Nietzsche: Decadence and Dionysian Faith*. Bloomington: Indiana University Press, 2008.

Birch, Charles. *On Purpose*. Sydney: New South Wales University Press, 1990.

Boda, Mark J., Daniel K. Fork, and Rodney A. Werline, Editors. *Seeking the Favor of God: Volume 3*, The Impact of Penitential Prayer beyond Second Temple Judaism. Atlanta GA: The Society of Biblical Literature, 2008.

Bohm, David. *Wholeness and the Implicate Order*. London: Routledge & Kegan Paul, 1980.

Bohm, David, and Basil J. Hiley. *The Undivided Universe: An Ontological Interpretation of Quantum Theory*. London: Routledge, 1993.

Bowlby, John. *Attachment and Loss*, Vol. 1, Attachment. New York: Basic Books, 1982.

Breighner, Russ. *Genesis, Faith, Science*. Pittsburgh, PA: Dorrance Publishing Co. Inc., 2012.

Brown, Alice. "Descartes's Dreams," *Journal of the Warburg and Courtauld Institutes*, 40, 1977.

Brown, Judith Anne. John Marco Allegro: *The Maverick of the Dead Sea Scrolls*. Michigan: W.B. Eerdmans Publishing Co., 2005.

Buber, Martin. *Hasidism and Modern Man*. New York: Horizon Press, 1958.

Caird, Edward. "Metaphysic," *Essays on Literature and Philosophy*, Vol. 2. Glasgow: MacLehose, 1892.

Campbell, Joseph. *Myths to Live By*. New York: Viking Press, 1972.

Caputo, John D. *The prayers and tears of Jacques Derrida: religion without religion*. Bloomington: Indiana University Press, 1997.

Chalmers, David J. "The Puzzle of Conscious Experience." *Scientific American*, 273, 1995

Chapman, Christopher N. *Freud, Religion, and Anxiety*. Morrisville NC: Lulu.com, 2007.

Chara, Paul and Jill N. Gillett. "Sensory Images of God: Divine Synesthesia?" *Journal of Psychology and Christianity*, 23, 3, 2004.

Clark, James M. and John V. Skinner, Editors and Translators. *Meister Eckhart: Selected Treatises and Sermons*. London: Faber & Faber, 1958.

Clark, J.M. *Meister Eckhart*. London: Nelson & Sons, 1957.

Clarke M, A. Lohan et al. "Genome of Acanthamoeba castellanii highlights extensive lateral gene transfer and early evolution of tyrosine kinase signalling." *Genome Biology*, 2013.

Corliss, William R. "Quantum mechanics is definitely spooky." *Science Frontiers* No. 114, Nov–Dec 1997.

Cornford, Francis M., Translator. *Plato's Theory of Knowledge*. New York: Dover Publications, 2003.

Cornford, Francis M., Translator. *Plato's Timaeus*. Edited by Oskar Piest. Indianapolis: Bobbs-Merrill, 1959.

Crossan, John Dominic. "Foreword," *A New New Testament: A Bible for the 21st Century Combining Traditional and Newly Discovered Texts*. Edited by Hal Taussig. Boston: Houghton Mifflin Harcourt, 2013.

Cupitt, Don. *Mysticism after Modernity*. Oxford: Blackwell, 1998.

D'Aquili, Eugene G. and Andrew P. Newberg. *The Mystical Mind: Probing the Biology of Religious Experience*. Minneapolis: Fortress Press, 1999.

David, Phillip. "The Wheel Broken at the Cistern: The Divergence of Orthodox Christianity from Gnosticism." *www.essene.com/*

EarlyChurch/OrthodoxFromGnostic/The_Wheel.htm.

Davies, Paul. *God and the New Physics*. London: Penguin Books Ltd., 1983.

Davies, Stevan. *The Gospel of Thomas: Annotated and Explained.* Woodstock, VT: SkyLight Paths Publishing, 2003.

De Landa, Manuel. *Intensive Science and Virtual Philosophy.* London: Continuum, 2004.

Deleuze, Gilles. "The Actual and the Virtual." In Gilles Deleuze and Claire Parnet, *Dialogues II*. Translated by Hugh Tomlinson and Barbara Habberjam. New York: Columbia University Press, 1987.

______ *Expressionism in Philosophy: Spinoza.* Translated by Martin Joughin. New York: Zone Books, 1990.

______ *Difference and Repetition*. Translated by Paul Patton. New York: Columbia University Press, 1994.

______ *Pure Immanence: Essays on a Life.* Translated by Anne Boyman. New York: Zone Books, 2001.

______ and Félix Guattari. *What Is Philosophy?* London: Verso, 1994.

Delio, Ilia. "Brain Science and the Biology of Belief: A Theological Response." *Zygon*, 38, 3, 2003.

Dennett, Daniel C. *Consciousness Explained.* Boston: Little, Brown and Company, 1991.

Derrida, Jacques. *"Différance."* In *Margins of Philosophy.* Translated by Alan Bass. Chicago: University of Chicago Press, 1982.

______ "How to avoid speaking: Denials" in *Derrida and Negative Theology.* Edited by Harold Coward and Toby Foshay. Albany: State University of New York Press, 1992.

______ *On the Name*. Edited and translated by Thomas Dutoit. Stanford: Stanford University Press, 1995.

______ *Responsibilities of Deconstruction.* Edited by Jonathon Dronsfield and Nick Midgley. Coventry: University of Warwick, 1997.

______ *Specters of Marx*. Translated by Peggy Kamuf. Abingdon, Oxon: Routledge, 1994.

Descartes, René, *Principles of Philosophy*, Translated by John Veitch. Montana: Kessinger Publishing. 2004.

_______ *Principles of Philosophy*. Translated by V. R. Miller and R.P. Miller. Dordrecht: Reidel, 1983. (Original Latin publication 1644).

Dominican Province, Translator. *Thomas Aquinas, Summa Theologica*: Vol. 1 of 10. Charleston SC, USA: Forgotten Books, 2007.

Dyson, Freeman. *Infinite in All Directions*. New York: Harper & Row, 1988.

Evans, C. de B., Editor and Translator. *Meister Eckhart by Franz Pfeiffer*. London: John M. Watkins, 1924.

Evans, William. *The Great Doctrines of the Bible*. Glendale, CA: Bibliotech Press, 2014.

Ewing, Alfred C. "Awareness of God." *Philosophy*, 40, no. 151, 1965.

Fakhry, Majid. "Three Varieties of Mysticism in Islam." *International Journal for Philosophy of Religion*, 2, no. 4, 1971.

Faust, Jennifer. "Can religious arguments persuade?". *International Journal for Philosophy of Religion*, 63, 2008.

Franks Davis, Caroline. *The Evidential Force of Religious Experience*. Oxford: Clarendon Press, 1989.

Friedman, Maurice S. *Martin Buber: The Life of Dialogue*. New York: Harpers, 1960.

Gonzáles, Alessandra L. "Measuring Religiosity in a Majority Muslim Context: Gender, Religious Salience and Religious Experience Among Kuwaiti College Students – A Research Note," *Journal for the Scientific Study of Religion*, 50, 2, 2011.

Goswami, Amit. "Physics within Nondual Consciousness." *Philosophy East and West*, 51, 4 2001.

Grandpierre, Attila. "Ultimate Reality and Meaning." *The Noetic Journal*, 23, 2000. www.mindspring.com/~noeticj.

Grof, Stanislav. *The Cosmic Game: Explorations in the Frontiers of Human Consciousness*. New York: State University of New York Press, 1998.

Guyer, Paul, Translator. *Notes and Fragments: The Cambridge Edition of the Works of Immanuel Kant*. New York: Cambridge University Press, 2005.

Hadi, Fawzyiah and Ghenaim Al-Fayez. "Islamic Arabic Youth and Family Development." *Handbook of Applied Developmental Science, 3*. Edited by Richard M. Lerner. Thousand Oaks, CA: Sage Publications Inc., 2003.

Hager, Lee. "The Gnostic Gospels: A Bridge between Science and Spirituality," 2011. *www.selfgrowth.com*.

Haldane, Elizabeth S. and G.R.T. Ross, Translators. "Rules for the Direction of the Mind," in *The Philosophical Works of Descartes,* 1911. Reprint Cambridge: Cambridge University Press, 1984.

Hall, A. Rupert and Marie Boas Hall, Editors. *Unpublished Scientific Papers of Isaac Newton.* Cambridge: Cambridge University Press, 1978.

Hart, James G. "Michel Henry's Phenomenological Theology of Life." *Husserl Studies,* Vol. 15, No. 2, October 1998.

____ *The Person and the Common Life.* Dordrecht: Kluwer, 1992.

____ "A Précis of an Husserlian Philosophical Theology," in *Essays in Phenomenological Theology.* Edited by Steven W. Laycock and James G. Hart. Albany: SUNY, 1986.

Hartshorne, Charles. *Omnipotence and other Theological Mistakes*. Albany: State University of New York Press, 1984.

Havel, Václav. "A sense of the transcendent," in *The Art of the Impossible: Politics as Morality in Practice*. New York: Knopf, 1997.

Hay, Louise L. *You Can Heal Your Life*. Carlsbad, CA: Hay House, 1984.

Heidegger, Martin. *An Introduction to Metaphysics*. Translated by Ralph Manhein. New Haven: Yale University Press, 1973.

______ *Being and Time*. Translated by John Macquarrie and Edward Robinson, Oxford: Blackwell, 1962.

______ *Contributions to Philosophy (From Enowning)*. Translated by Parvis Emad and Kenneth Maly. Bloomington: Indiana University Press, 1999.

______ *Early Greek Thinking*. Translated by David F. Krell and F.A. Capuzzi. New York: Harper & Row, 1975.

______ "Letter on Humanism." *Martin Heidegger: Basic Writings.* Edited by David F. Krell New York: Harper & Row, 1977.

______ "What is Metaphysics?" *Martin Heidegger: Pathmarks.* Edited by William McNeill. Cambridge: Cambridge University Press, 1998.

Hick, John. *God Has Many Names*. Louisville: Westminster John Knox Press, 2000.

Hiley, Basil J. "Process and the Implicate Order: their relevance to Quantum Theory and Mind," *http://www.ctr4process.org/publications/Articles/LSI05/Hiley%20paper.pdf.*

Hoffman, Edward. *The way of splendor: Jewish Mysticism and Modern Psychology*. Lanham, MD: Rowman & Littlefield Publishers Inc., 2007.

Hong Howard and Edna Hong, Editors and Translators. *Søren Kierkegaard's Journals and Papers*. Bloomington, Indiana: Indiana University Press, 1967–1978.

Hooge, J. Rosalie. *Providential Beginnings*. Maitland, FL: Xulon Press, 2003.

Hubble, Edwin. "A Relation between Distance and Radial Velocity among Extra-Galactic Nebulae." *Proceedings of the National Academy of Sciences of the United States of America* 15, no.3, 1929.

Hume, David. *Dialogues Concerning Natural Religion* (1779) in: *Dialogues and Natural History of Religion.* Edited by J.A.C. Gaskin. Oxford & New York: Oxford University Press, 1993.

_____ *Enquiry Concerning Human Understanding*. Edited by L.A. Selby-Bigge. Oxford: Oxford University Press, 1966.

_____ *Philosophical essays: on morals, literature, and politics, Volume II*. Philadelphia: Edward Earle, 1817, Section X.

_____ *The Philosophical Works of David Hume,* Vol. I. Edinburgh: Adam Black and William Tate, 1826.

_____ *A Treatise of Human Nature*. Edited by L. A. Selby-Bigge, 2nd ed. revised by P.H. Nidditch. Oxford: Clarendon Press, 1975.

Hunt, Tam. "Absent-Minded Science – Part I." *Noetic Now,* 4, 2010.

Husserl, Edmund. "Correspondence to Arnold Metzger." *Husserl: Shorter Works*. Edited by Peter McCormick and Frederick Elliston. Notre Dame, Indiana: University of Notre Dame Press, 1981.

_____ *The Crisis of European Sciences and Transcendental Phenomenology*. Translated by D. Carr. Evanston, Illinois: Northwestern University Press, 1970.

_____ Essays and lectures. 1922–1937. Edited by T. Nenon H.R. Sepp. The Hague, Netherlands: Kluwer Academic Publishers, 1988.

_____ *Ideas Pertaining to a Pure Phenomenology and to a Phenomenological Philosophy, First Book*. Translated by F. Kersten. Dordrecht: Kluwer, 1983.

Husserl Manuscripts, Leuven, Belgium. Ms A V 21; Ms E III 4; Ms E III 9.

Iqbal, Muhammad. "The Reconstruction of Religious Thought in Islam." Edited by M. Saeed Sheikh. Lahore: Institute of Islamic Culture, 1996. Cited in Mohammad Iqbal Afaqi, "Knowledge, Belief and Faith: A Comparative Study of Christian and Islamic Epistemologies," PhD dissertation submitted to The University of the Punjab, Lahore, 2003.

Jacobs, Louis. *A Jewish Theology*. Springfield, NJ: Behrman House Inc., 1973.

James, William. *Essays in Radical Empiricism*. New York: Cosimo Inc., 2008.

_____ *The Varieties of Religious Experience: A Study in Human Nature*. New York: Longmans, Green, and Co., 1902.

_____ *The Will to Believe and Other Essays in Popular Philosophy*. New York: Cosimo, Inc., 2007.

Jaworski, Joseph. *Source: The Inner Path of Knowledge Creation*. San Francisco: Berrett-Koehler Publishers, Inc., 2012.

Jestice, Phyllis G. *Holy People of the World: A Cross-Cultural Encyclopedia*. Santa Barbara, CA: ABC-CLIO Inc., 2004.

Kant, Immanuel. *The Conflict of the Faculties*. Translated by Mary J. Gregor. New York: Abaris Books, 1992.

____ A Critical Inquiry into Grounds of Proof for the Existence of God. *Metaphysical works of the celebrated Immanuel Kant*. Translated by John Richardson. London: W. Simpkin & R. Marshall, 1836.

_____ *Critique of Judgment*. Translated by John H. Bernard. New York: Cosimo Inc., 2007.

_____ *The Critique of Practical Reason*. Translated by Thomas Kingsmill Abbott. New York: Barnes & Noble Publishing, 2004.

_____ *The Critique of Pure Reason*. Translated by J.M.D. Meiklejohn. Radford, VA: Wilder Publications, 2008.

_____ *Lectures on Ethics*. Translated by L. Infield. London: Methuen, 1979.

_____ *Opus postumum*. Edited by Eckart Förster. Translated by Eckart Förster and Michael Rosen. Cambridge: Cambridge University Press, 1993.

Kaufman, Walter, Editor and Translator. *The Portable Nietzsche*. New York: Penguin Books, 1954.

Kavanaugh, Leslie Jaye. *The Architectonic of Philosophy: Plato, Aristotle, Leibniz*. Amsterdam: Amsterdam University Press, 2007.

Khan, Pir Vilayat Inayat. "Toward a Unified Worldview: New Perspectives in Science & Spirituality." *www.embracingthecontradiction.org/unified.htm*.

Kierkegaard, Søren. *Sickness Unto Death*. Radford VA: A & D Publishing, 2008.

Kirkpatrick, Lee A. "A Longitudinal Study of Changes in Religious Belief and Behavior as a Function of Individual Differences in Adult Attachment Style." *Journal for the Scientific Study of Religion*, 36, no.2, 1997.

_____ *Attachment, evolution, and the psychology of religion*. New York: Guilford Press, 2005.

_____ "The role of attachment in religious belief and behavior." *Advances in Personal Relationships*, vol. 5. Edited by Daniel Perlman and Kim Bartholomew. London: Jessica Kingsley, 1994.

_____ and Phillip R. Shaver. "Attachment Theory and Religion: Childhood Attachments, Religious Experience, and Conversion." *Journal for the Scientific Study of Religion*, 29, 3, 1990.

Kramer, Kenneth Paul. *Martin Buber's I and Thou: practising living dialogue*. Mahwah, NU: Paulist Press, 2003.

Krell, David F., Editor. "Letter on Humanism." *Martin Heidegger: Basic Writings*. New York: Harper & Row, 1977.

Kumari, Anupam and R. S. Pirta. "Exploring Human Relationship with God as a Secure Base." *Journal of the Indian Academy of Applied Psychology*, 35, October 2009.

Lamm, Norman. *The Religious Thought of Hasidism: Text and Commentary*. Hoboken, NJ: KTAV Publishing House Inc., 1999.

LaViolette, Paul A. *Subquantum Kinetics: A Systems Approach*. Niskayuna, NY: Starlane Publications, 2010.

Leaman, Oliver, Editor. *Encyclopedia of Asian Philosophy*. New York: Routledge, 2001.

Leibniz, Gottfried Wilhelm. *The Monadology and other philosophical writings*. New York: Garland Publishing Inc., 1985.

______ *Discourse on Metaphysics and the Monadology*. New York: Cosimo, 2008.

Lings, Martin. *A Sufi Saint of the Twentieth Century*. London: George Allen & Unwin Ltd., 1971.

______*What is Sufism*? Berkeley: University of California Press, 1975.

Locke, John. *A Letter on Toleration*. Edited by James H. Tully. Translated by William Popple, Indianapolis: Hackett, 1983.

_____ *An Essay Concerning Human Understanding*. Edited by Peter H. Niddich. Oxford: Oxford University Press, 1979.

_____ "The Reasonableness of Christianity." *The Works of John Locke* Vol. VII. London: Otridge & Son et al., 1812.

McGinn, Colin. *The Problem of Consciousness: Essays Toward a Resolution*. Malden, MA: Blackwell, 1991.

McMahon, John H., Translator. *The Metaphysics of Aristotle* Book I, Ch. III. London: Henry G. Bohn, 1857.

McTaggart, Lynne. *The Field: The Quest for the Secret Force of the Universe*. London: HarperCollins, 2009.

Mall, R.A. "The God of phenomenology in comparative contrast to that of philosophy and Theology." *Husserl Studies*, 8, 1991.

Mander, William. "Edward Caird and British Idealist Philosophy," address given at Oxford University, 20 January 1998.

Margulis, Lynn and Dorian Sagan. *Microcosmos: Four Billion Years from Our Microbial Ancestors*. New York: Simon & Schuster, 1986.

Marion, Jean-Luc. "The Banality of Saturation." Translated by Jeffrey L. Kosky. *Counter-Experiences*. Edited by Kevin Hart. Notre Dame, Indiana: University of Notre Dame Press, 2007.

_____ *Communio*. Edited by Jean-Luc Marion and Hans Urs von Balthasar. Cited in Emmanuel Falque, "Larvatus pro Deo." Translated by Robyn Horner. Counter-Experiences. Edited by Kevin Hart. Notre Dame, Indiana: University of Notre Dame Press, 2007.

_____ *God Without Being*. Translated by Thomas A. Carlson. Chicago: University of Chicago Press, 1995.

_____ *The Idol and Distance,* Translated by Thomas A. Carlson. New York: Fordham University Press, 2001.

_____ *In Excess: Studies of Saturated Phenomena.* Translated by Robyn Horner and Vincent Berraud. New York: Fordham University Press, 2002.

_____ "In the Name: How to Avoid Speaking of 'Negative Theology.'" *God, the Gift and Postmodernism.* Edited by John D. Caputo and Michael J. Scanlon. Bloomington: Indiana University Press, 1999.

_____ "Metaphysics and Phenomenology: A Relief for Theology." Translated by Thomas A. Carlson. *Critical Inquiry,* 20, 4, 1994.

_____ "They recognized him; And he became invisible to them." *Modern Theology,* 18, 2002.

_____ *The Visible and the Revealed.* Translated by Christina M. Gschwandtner. New York: Fordham University Press, 2008.

Maslim, Audrey A. and Jeffrey P. Bjorck. "Reasons for Conversion to Islam Among Women in the United States." *Psychology of Religion and Spirituality,* 1, no. 2, 2009.

Maslow, Abraham H. *Religions, Values, and Peak Experiences.* London: Penguin Books, 1976.

Masood, Steven. "Wahdat al-Wujud: a fundamental doctrine in Sufism." *www.stevenmasood.org/articles/Wahdat.html.*

Matt, Daniel C. *The Essential Kabbalah.* San Francisco: Harper, 1995.

Michaelson, Jay. *Everything Is God: The Radical Path of Nondual Judaism.* Boston: Shambalah Publications Inc., 2009.

Mikulincer, Mario and Phillip R. Shaver. *Attachment in Adulthood.* New York: Guilford Publications, Inc., 2007.

Miller, Jonathan Scott. "Are Mystical Experiences Evidence for the Existence of a Transcendent Reality? Evaluating Eugene d'Aquili and Andrew Newberg's Argument for Absolute Unitary Being." *Florida Philosophical Review,* IX, no.1, 2009.

Min, Anselm K. "Naming the Unnameable God: Levinas, Derrida, and Marion." *International Journal for Philosophy of*

Religion, 60, no. 1/3, 2006.

More, Śesharāva. *Islam, maker of the Muslim mind*. Pune, India: Rajhans Prakashan, 2004.

Mortensen, Viggo, Editor. *Theology and the Religions: A Dialogue.*, Michigan: Wm. B. Eerdmans Publishing Co., 2003.

Murrell, Beatrix. "The Cosmic Plenum: Bohm's Gnosis: The Implicate Order." *www.bizcharts.com/stoa_del_sol/plenum/plenum_3.html*

Nadeau, Robert and Menas Kafatos, *The Non-Local Universe: The New Physics and Matters of the Mind*. Oxford: Oxford University Press, 1999.

Neaman, Judith S. "Potentiation, Elevation, Acceleration: Prerogatives of Women Mystics," *Mystics Quarterly*, 14, 1, 1988.

Newberg, Andrew and Mark Robert Waldman, *Why We Believe What We Believe*. New York: Free Press, 2006.

Newberg, Andrew, Eugene d'Aquili, and Vince Rause, *Why God Won't Go Away: Brain Science and the Biology of Belief*. New York, Ballantine Books, 2002.

Nicholi, Armand M. "A new dimension of youth culture," *American Journal of Psychiatry*, 131, 1974.

Nietzsche, Friedrich. *Beyond Good & Evil*. Translated by M. Faber. Oxford: Oxford University Press, 1998.

______ *The Gay Science*. Edited by Bernard Williams. Cambridge: Cambridge University Press, 2003.

______ *Human, All Too Human*. Translated by Gary Handwerk. Stanford: Stanford University Press, 1997.

______ "Morality as Anti-Nature." *Twilight of the Idols*. New York: Oxford University Press, 1998.

______ *On the Genealogy of Morals Essay II*. Translated by Walter Kaufmann and R. J. Hollingdale. New York: Random House, 1967.

______ *On the Genealogy of Morals*. Translated by Carol Diethe. Cambridge: Cambridge University Press, 1994.

______ "To the Unknown God." Cited in Bruce Ellis Bension, *Pious Nietzsche: Decadence and Dionysian Faith*. Bloomington: Indiana University Press, 2008.

______ *Thus Spoke Zarathustra*. Edited by Adrian Del Caro and Robert Pippin, Cambridge: Cambridge University Press, 2006.

______ *The Twilight of the Idols and The Antichrist*. Translated by Thomas Common. Digireads.com Publishing, 2009.

Novak, David, and Randi Rashkover, *Tradition in the Public Square: A David Novak Reader.* Norwich: SCM Press, 2008.

Oppenheim, Michael. "The Meaning of Hasidut: Martin Buber and Gershom Scholem." *Journal of the American Academy of Religion*, 49, 3, 1981.

Outler, Alberg C., Editor and Translator. *Saint Augustine: Confessions and Enchiridion.* Louisville, KY: Westminster John Knox Press, 1955.

Pagels, Elaine. *Beyond Belief: The Secret Gospel of Thomas*. New York: Random House, 2003.

_____ *The Gnostic Gospels*. New York: Vintage Books, 1979.

Panella, John V. *The Gnostic Papers: The Undiscovered Mysteries of Christ*. Huntsville, AR: Ozark Mountain Publishers, 2002.

Pangle, Thomas L. *The Laws of Plato*. Chicago: University of Chicago Press, 1988.

Pascal, Blaise. *Pensées*. Translated by A.J. Krailsheimer. London: Penguin Books, 1966.

Peacocke, Arthur. "The Sound of Sheer Silence: How Does God Communicate with Humanity?" *Neuroscience and the Person: Scientific Perspectives on Divine Action*. Edited by Robert John Russell. Notre Dame, IN: University of Notre Dame Press, 1999.

Peat, F. David, Editor. *The Pari Dialogues: Essays in Science, Religion, Society and the Arts*. Grosetto, Italy: Pari Publishing, 2007.

Peperzak, Adriaan T. "Affective Theology, Theological

Affectivity." *Religious Experience and the End of Metaphysics*. Edited by Jeffrey Bloechl. Bloomington: Indiana University Press, 2003.

Persinger, Michael. "Experimental Simulation of the God Experience: Implications for Religious Beliefs and the Future of the Human Species." *Neurotheology: Brain, Science, Spirituality, Religious Experience*. Edited by Rhawn Joseph. San Jose, CA: University of California Press, 2002.

_____ *Neuropsychological Bases of God Beliefs*. New York: Praeger Publishers, 1987.

Peterson, Gregory R. "Mysterium Tremendum." *Zygon*, 37, 2, 2002.

Plantinga, Alvin. "Is Belief in God Properly Basic? *Noûs*, 15, no. 1, 1981.

Planck, Max. *The Observer*, January 25, 1931.

Pratt, David. "The Monistic Idealism of A. Goswami." *davidpratt.info/goswami.htm*.

Proudfoot, Wayne. *Religious Experience*. Berkeley: University of California Press, 1985.

Pylkkkänen, Paavo. *Mind, Matter, and the Implicate Order*. New York: Springer, 2007.

Qutb, Syed. Commentary on Surah 103 – The Declining Day a'Asr. *web.youngmuslims.ca/online_library/tafsir/syed_qutb/surah_103.htm*.

Rahman, Fazlur. *Islam*. London: University of Chicago press, 1979.

Ratcliffe, Matthew. "Neurotheology: A Science of What?" *The Neurology of Religious Experience*. Edited by Patrick McNamara. Portsmouth, NH: Greenwood Publishing Group Inc., 2006.

Roberts, Catherine. "Insight in Science and in Plato." *Manas Journal*, xxxvi, 9, 1983.

Robinson, J.M., Editor. *Nag Hammadi Library* 121, 24. Cited in Elaine Pagels, *Beyond Belief: The Secret Gospel of Thomas*. New

York: Random House, 2003. (The English translation is by Pagels.)

Rogers, Peter C. *Universal Truth: Thinking outside the Box: Book II*. Bloomington, IN: Author House, 2011.

Rorty, Richard. "Anti-clericalism and atheism." *Religion After Metaphysics*. Mark A. Wrathall. Cambridge: Cambridge University Press, 2003.

Ross, Gilliam. *Psyche's Yearning: Radical Perspectives on Self Transformation*. Bloomington, IN: Trafford Publishing, 2010.

Runehov, Anne L.C. *Sacred or Neural? The Potential of Neuroscience to Explain Religious Experience*. Göttingen: Vandenhoeck & Ruprecht, 2007.

Samanta-Laughton, Manjir. *Punk Science: Inside the Mind of God*. Winchester, UK: O Books, 2006.

Schaff, Philip, Editor. *Nicene and Post-Nicene Fathers*, vol. 9. Grand Rapids, Mich.: Eerdmans, 1981.

Schimmel, Annemarie. *Islam in the Indian Subcontinent*. Leiden, The Netherlands: E. J. Brill, 1980.

Scholem, Gershom. "How I Came to the Kabbalah." *Commentary*, 69, 1980.

Schorsch, Ismar. "The Sacred Cluster: The Core Values of Conservative Judaism," 1995. *www.jewishvirtuallibrary.org/.../Judaism/conservative_values.html*.

Schwartz, Arthur J. "The Nature of Spiritual Transformation: A Review of the Literature," 2000. *www.metanexus.net/archive/spiritualtransformationresearch/research/pdf/STSRP-LiteratureReview2-7.PDF*.

Shah-Kazemi, Reza. *Paths to Transcendence: According to Shankara, Ibn Arabi, and Meister Eckhart*. Bloomington: World Wisdom Inc., 2006.

Sobottka, Stanley. "The three major metaphysical philosophies." Charlottesville, VA: University of Virginia, 2010. *faculty.virginia.edu/consciousness/new_page_4.htm*.

Stace, W.T. *Mysticism and Philosophy*. London: Macmillan, 1960.

Stapp, Henry P. "Why Classical Mechanics Cannot Naturally Accommodate Consciousness But Quantum Mechanics Can," 2008. *http://arxiv.org/pdf/quant-ph/9502012vl.pdf.*

Steinhardt Paul J. and Neil Turok, *Endless Universe: Beyond the Big Bang – Rewriting Cosmic History*. New York: Broadway Books, 2007.

Strawson, Galen. "Realistic monism: why physicalism entails panpsychism." *Journal of Consciousness Studies,* 13, 2006.

Swinburne, Richard. *The Existence of God*. Oxford: Clarendon Press, 1979.

Tillich, Paul. *Systematic Theology,* Vol. 1. Chicago: University of Chicago Press, 2012.

Touger, Rabbi Eliyahu, Translator. "A Knowing Heart." Sichos In Which The Rebbe Advanced Our Emotional Frontiers, from *The Works of The Lubavitcher Rebbe, Rabbi Menachem M. Schneerson*. New York: Sichos In English, 2002.

Trakakis, Nick, Editor. *William L. Rowe on Philosophy of Religion: Selected Writings*. Aldershot, Hampshire: Ashgate Publishing Limited, 2007.

Turner, Denys. "Tradition and Faith," *International Journal of Systematic Theology,* 6, 1, 2004.

_____ *The Darkness of God: Negativity in Christian Mysticism*. Cambridge: Cambridge University Press, 1995.

Turner, Michael S. "Cosmology Solved? Quite Possibly!". *Publications of the Astronomical Society of the Pacific,* Vol. 111, no. 757, March 1999.

Van Nieuwenhuijze, C.A.O. "Religion versus Science in Islam: A Past and Future Question," *Die Welt des Islams,* New Series, 33, 2, 1993.

Weber, Marianne. *Max Weber: A biography*. New Brunswick, N.J.: Transaction, 1988. Cited in William H. Swatos, Jr. and Peter Kivisto, "Max Weber as 'Christian Sociologist'". *Journal for the Scientific Study of Religion,* 30, 4, 1991.

Weber, Renée. "Field Consciousness and Field Ethics." *Re-*

Vision, Summer/Fall 1978.

_____ *Dialogues with Scientists and Sages*. London: Routledge & Kegan Paul, 1986.

Whitehead, Alfred North. *Process and Reality*. New York: Macmillan, 1929.

Williams, Bernard. "Deciding to believe." *Problems of the Self*. New York: Cambridge, 1973.

Wright, Jonathan. *Heretics: The Creation of Christianity from the Gnostics to the Modern Church*. New York: Houghton Mifflin Harcourt Publishing Company, 2011.

Wright, Sewald. "Panpsychism and Science." *Mind in Nature: Essays on the Interface of Science and Philosophy*. Edited by J.B. Cobb and D.R. Griffin. Lanham, MD: University Press of America, 1977.

Yandell, Keith E. *The Epistemology of Religious Experience*. Cambridge: Cambridge University Press, 1993.

Zajonc, Arthur. "New Wine in What Kind of Wineskins? Metaphysics in the Twenty-First Century," *New Metaphysical Foundations of Modern Science*. Edited by Willis Harman and Jane Clark. Sausalito, CA: Institute of Noetic Sciences, 1994.

Zangwill, Nick. "The myth of religious experience." *Religious Studies*, 40, 2004.

Zinnbauer, Brian J. and Kenneth I. Pargament. "Spiritual Conversion: A Study of Religious Change Among College Students." *Journal for the Scientific Study of Religion*, 37, 1, 1998.

Zohar, Danah and Ian Marshall. *SQ: Connecting with Our Spiritual Intelligence*. London: Bloomsbury Publishing Plc., 2001.

THE NEW OPEN SPACES

Throughout the two thousand years of Christian tradition there have been, and still are, groups and individuals that exist in the margins and upon the edge of faith. But in Christianity's contrapuntal history it has often been these outcasts and pioneers that have forged contemporary orthodoxy out of former radicalism as belief evolves to engage with and encompass the ever-changing social and scientific realities. Real faith lies not in the comfortable certainties of the Orthodox, but somewhere in a half-glimpsed hinterland on the dirt track to Emmaus, where the Death of God meets the Resurrection, where the supernatural Christ meets the historical Jesus, and where the revolution liberates both the oppressed and the oppressors.

Welcome to Christian Alternative... a space at the edge where the light shines through.

If you have enjoyed this book, why not tell other readers by posting a review on your preferred book site.

Recent bestsellers from Christian Alternative are:

Bread Not Stones

The Autobiography of An Eventful Life

Una Kroll

The spiritual autobiography of a truly remarkable woman and a history of the struggle for ordination in the Church of England.

Paperback: 978-1-78279-804-0 ebook: 978-1-78279-805-7

The Quaker Way

A Rediscovery

Rex Ambler

Although fairly well known, Quakerism is not well understood. The purpose of this book is to explain how Quakerism works as a spiritual practice.

Paperback: 978-1-78099-657-8 ebook: 978-1-78099-658-5

Blue Sky God

The Evolution of Science and Christianity

Don MacGregor

Quantum consciousness, morphic fields and blue-sky thinking about God and Jesus the Christ.

Paperback: 978-1-84694-937-1 ebook: 978-1-84694-938-8

Celtic Wheel of the Year

Tess Ward

An original and inspiring selection of prayers combining Christian and Celtic Pagan traditions, and interweaving their calendars into a single pattern of prayer for every morning and night of the year.

Paperback: 978-1-90504-795-6

Christian Atheist

Belonging without Believing

Brian Mountford

Christian Atheists don't believe in God but miss him: especially the transcendent beauty of his music, language, ethics, and community.

Paperback: 978-1-84694-439-0 ebook: 978-1-84694-929-6

Compassion Or Apocalypse?

A Comprehensible Guide to the Thoughts of René Girard

James Warren

How René Girard changes the way we think about God and the Bible, and its relevance for our apocalypse-threatened world.

Paperback: 978-1-78279-073-0 ebook: 978-1-78279-072-3

Diary Of A Gay Priest

The Tightrope Walker

Rev. Dr. Malcolm Johnson

Full of anecdotes and amusing stories, but the Church is still a dangerous place for a gay priest.

Paperback: 978-1-78279-002-0 ebook: 978-1-78099-999-9

Do You Need God?

Exploring Different Paths to Spirituality Even For Atheists

Rory J.Q. Barnes

An unbiased guide to the building blocks of spiritual belief.

Paperback: 978-1-78279-380-9 ebook: 978-1-78279-379-3

Readers of ebooks can buy or view any of these bestsellers by clicking on the live link in the title. Most titles are published in paperback and as an ebook. Paperbacks are available in traditional bookshops. Both print and ebook formats are available online.

Find more titles and sign up to our readers' newsletter at http://www.johnhuntpublishing.com/christianity
Follow us on Facebook at
https://www.facebook.com/ChristianAlternative